Fractal Art

Andrew Shecktor

Author Biography, Andrew Shecktor

Born in 1956 in Philadelphia, and currently residing in Berwick Pennsylvania in the heart of coal country, Andrew Shecktor has authored a number of short manuscripts and articles of fiction and non-fiction over his 40 year part time writing career. He worked as a technical writer for ECRI, a medical device evaluation firm in Plymouth Meeting, PA. He assisted his mother, Maria C. Shecktor (deceased), published author of children's books, with her adult class on creative writing. She has been his inspiration for his writings and for the writing of this novel. He is a self-taught fine artist in oil, acrylic and pastel, and is a member of the North Mountain Art League. He is also an amateur photographer, an art he learned from his father, Fred Kerek Shecktor (deceased), who was the public relations director for the city of Philadelphia in the 1960's and a professional photographer for Merck Pharmaceuticals. Fred was also a press photographer for the "Philadelphia Record" newspaper in the 1950's.

When the author asked his father for a good camera, like the ones he used, so he could learn photography, his father replied, "I'll get you a Brownie box camera, and when you can take good pictures with that, I'll buy you any camera you want." After a number of years, and some award winning photos with that Brownie camera, his father made good on that promise, thus proving his point that anyone can take pictures but not everyone is a photographer. The art is in the composition and planning, and in making the best use of the equipment at hand.

The author is an electrical engineer by trade and has worked as a biomedical equipment engineer in charge of several major city hospitals. Recently he has worked in the computer industry and website services. He has also been involved in the political arena both as support staff and as a candidate for office. He has a keen interest in ghost hunting and the study of scientific anomalies. He is a fine artist in oil, pastel, acrylic, and watercolor, and specializes in putting art on unique media. He developed an interest in fractal art after working with fractal equations during an engineering project in the mid 1990's. A friend pointed out how artists were using fractals and computers to generate sophisticated works of art, many even appearing in fine art galleries in New York. Thus began his journey into math as art. Most of his fractal art he prints on glass, acrylic, or metal. Glass in particular brings out the beauty of the fractal, and a number of companies now specialize in printing on these media.

In the spring of 2014 he published his first short novel, "Centralia PA, Devils Fire." The novel is a unique combination of history and fiction, including metaphorical demons being battled by metaphorical heroes that represent the battle between the poor, overworked coal miner and the wealthy, greedy mine owners and operators. The book is currently on sale online and at a number of local venues in and around Centralia, in bookstores and online. The author is currently a member of the "North Mountain Art League" and displays his works at a number of league sponsored events.

What is a fractal?

A fractal is a never ending pattern that repeats itself at different scales. Complex fractals are created by the repetition of a simple mathematical process.

Fractals occur in nature in seashells, branches of trees, lightning, galaxies in space, hurricanes, and in the very structure of neurons in the brain and blood vessels in the body.

There are many mathematical formulations for fractals, most notably the Mandelbrot set, where a simple calculation is repeated many times with the result of the equation being used as the "seed" for the next one (the fractal equation contains one or more variables which are seeded initially.)

The results of a fractal calculation can be described graphically, and can be wonderfully beautiful. Some fractal artists create fractal videos, which represent either the zooming into a fractal image or the actual creation of the fractal as it runs through its calculations.

Fractal calculations are used in the creation of some computer generated imagery used in the motion picture industry. Fractal art has been around for some time, and many of the current programs are derivatives of early PC software from the 1990's. Only recently has computing power grown to the point where intricate fractal images can be produced fairly quickly, and moving image videos can be created. Even so, some fractals take time to calculate. On a dual core or four core processor an intricate fractal image can take up to an hour to render. Simpler images render in less than 10 minutes (and pretty much eat up all the processing power available.) It will be interesting to see what future, faster computing systems will be able to produce.

There is much information available on the Internet, and there are many free software programs and apps available for those who want to experiment with fractals.

I personally use a number of programs, and find it easier to create art on a "real" computer with a large monitor (as opposed to a tablet or smart phone.)

Some of the software programs I find best for fractal art are "Mandelbulb 3D", Apophasis, Chaoscope, Frost, Sterling, Apophysis and JWildfire. In addition, a good photo editing program is useful to combine images and tweak the final color. "IrfanView" is a good free alternative to "Photoshop" and can use Photoshop filters (Photoshop has out priced itself since it went on a monthly subscription basis and is now being shunned by most occasional users who typically buy last year's product and keep it for a number of years - you can't do this with a monthly subscription product.)

I use JWildfire and Frost heavily, sometimes blending or augmenting images from both programs. Plugins are available that will simplify visual manipulation and usually offer user defined parameters.

Once you have created a fractal image you can print it or use it for a background for websites or print. Additionally, you can add photographic or other elements, or combine fractal images to create a unique artistic image. There are a number of wonderful ways to display fractal art. I find that printing on glass, acrylic, and metal bring out the colors and contrast far better than printing on paper.

This book presents some of the fractal images I have created. I like to keep my images simple, but if you search the Internet you can find some quite intricate examples of fractal imaging.

I wish to thank all those who pioneered the science of fractal art as well as those who dedicated the time and effort to create the numerous fractal art software programs and algorithms and who have offered their knowledge and software free of charge in most cases. Their hard work has provided the framework that brought fractals from hardcore mathematics to an art form. With a bit of imagination and a bit of mathematics today's fractal artist can create unique and exquisite images that were not possible before the invention of the personal computer.

I hope you enjoy these images and pursue further research into the wonders of fractals!

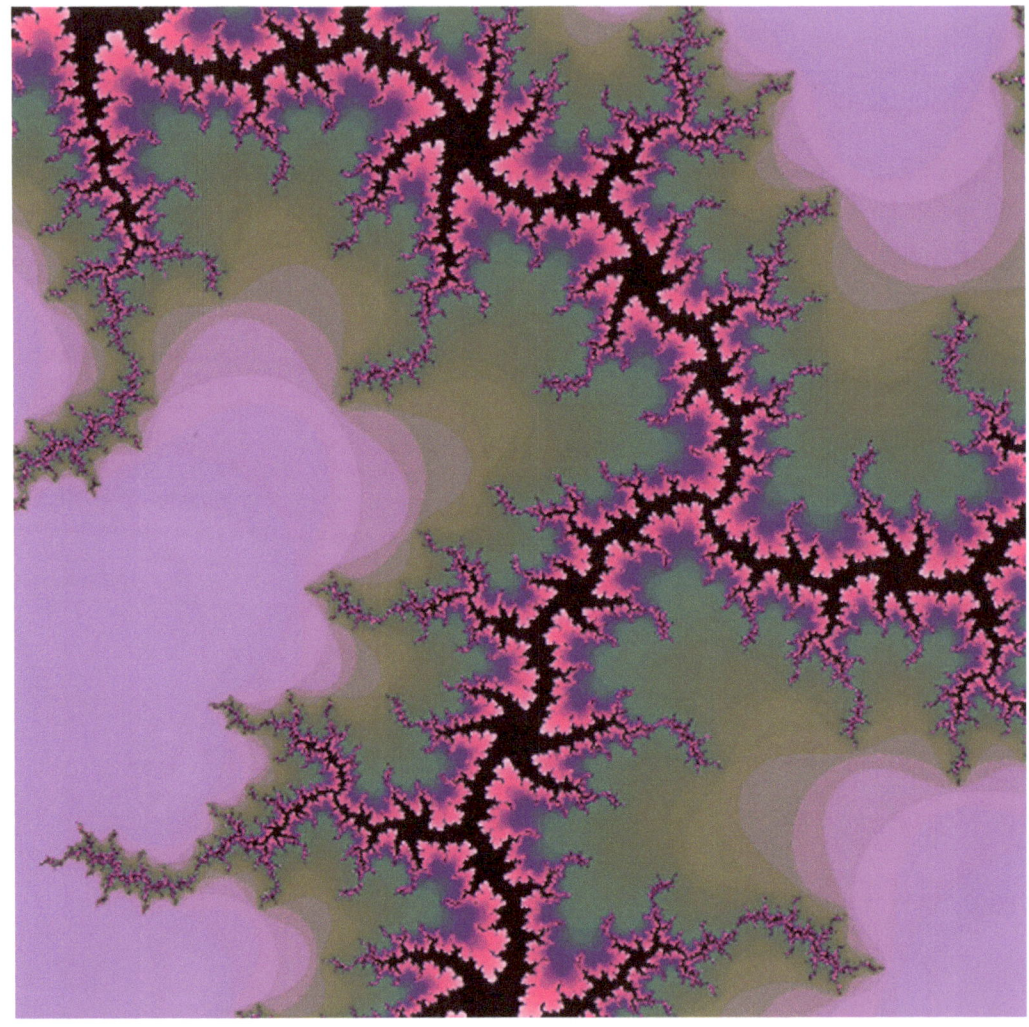

Basic Mandelbrot fractal image, zoomed about 1000 times. When you create a Mandelbrot fractal you can zoom into any section. Though the equations repeat, the results are slightly different each time, and the images change as you "drill down" into the fractal.

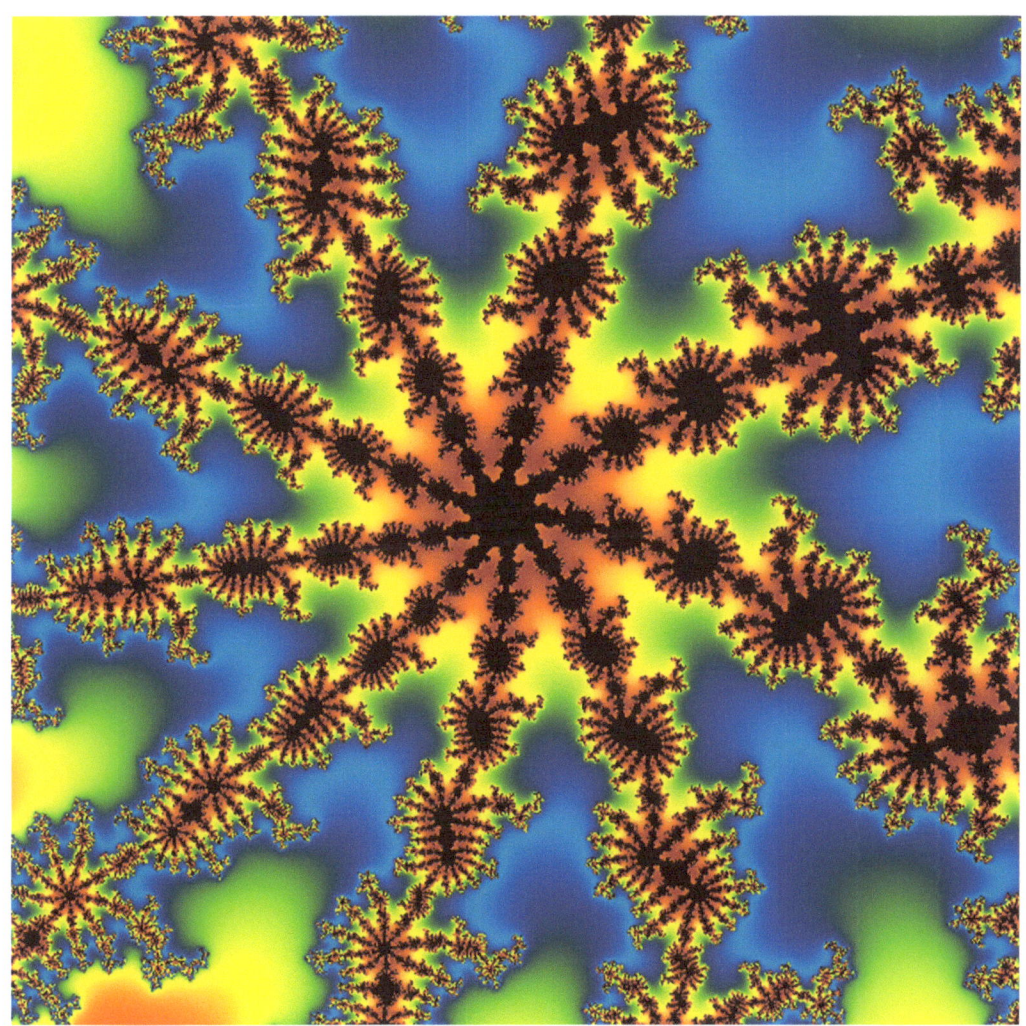

Another basic Mandelbrot fractal, zoomed in about 100 times.

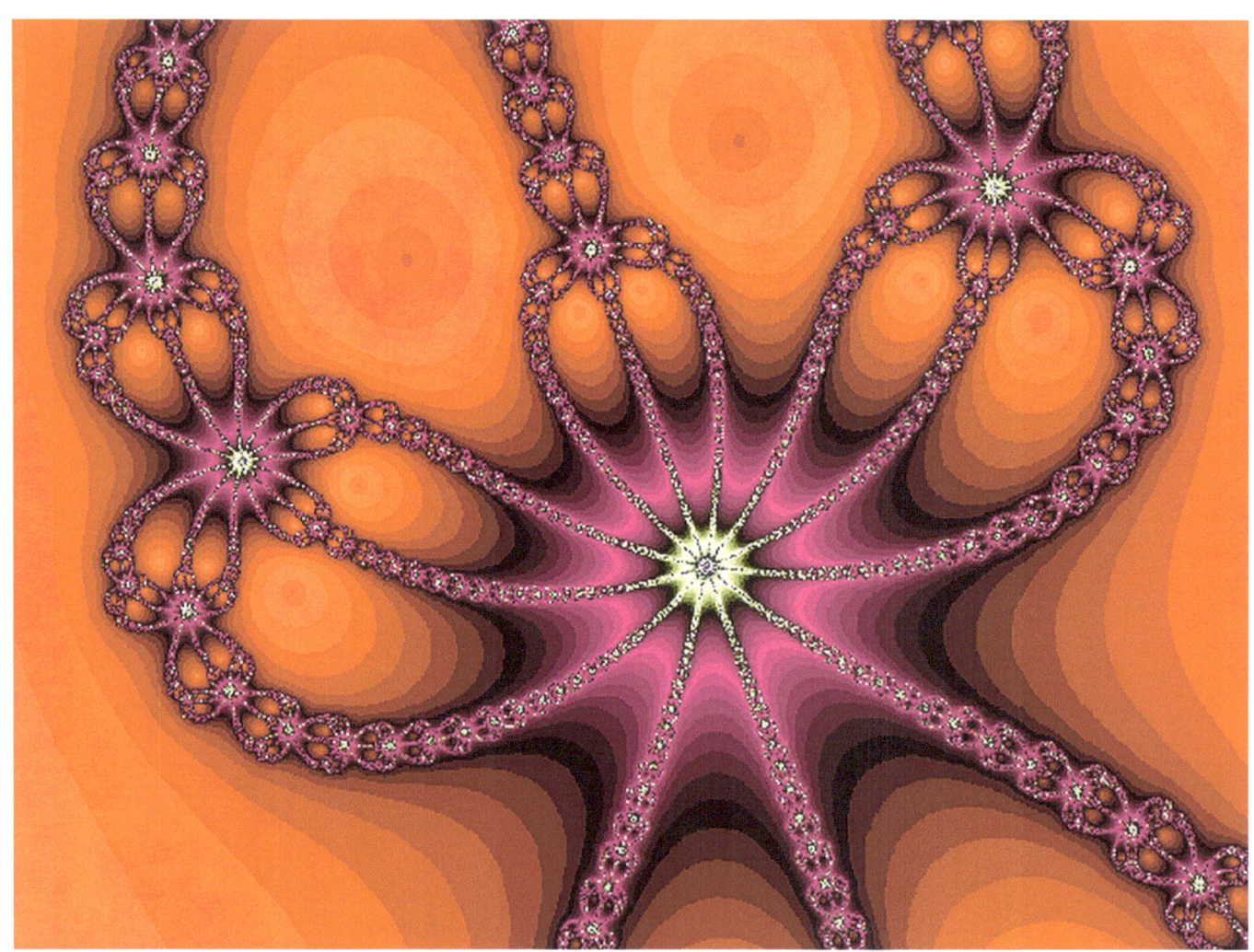

A slightly more sophisticated Mandelbrot fractal. This one is a third order derivative.

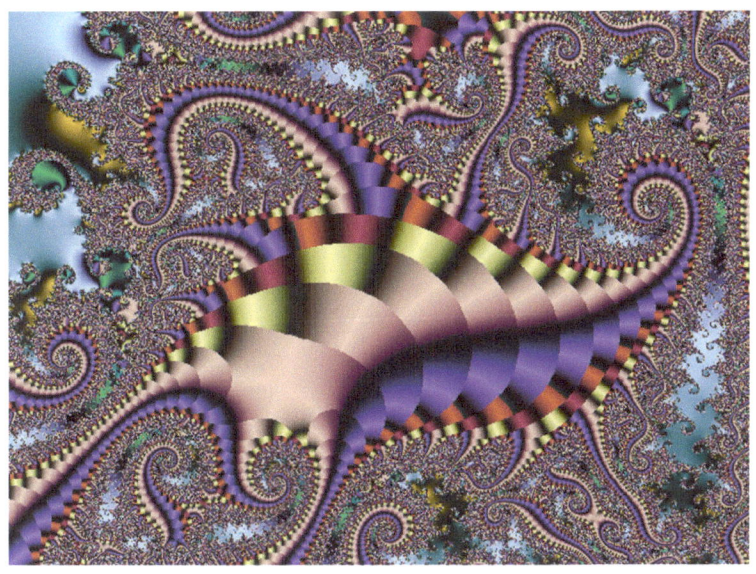

A couple more generic Mandelbrot fractals

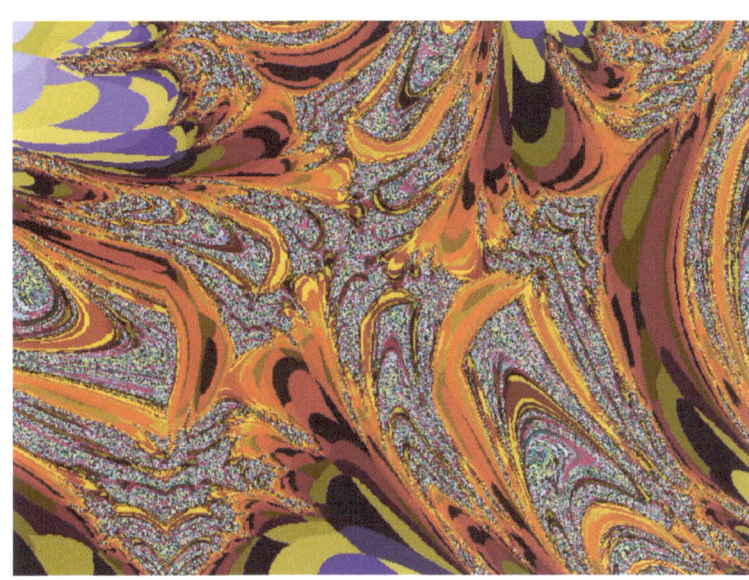

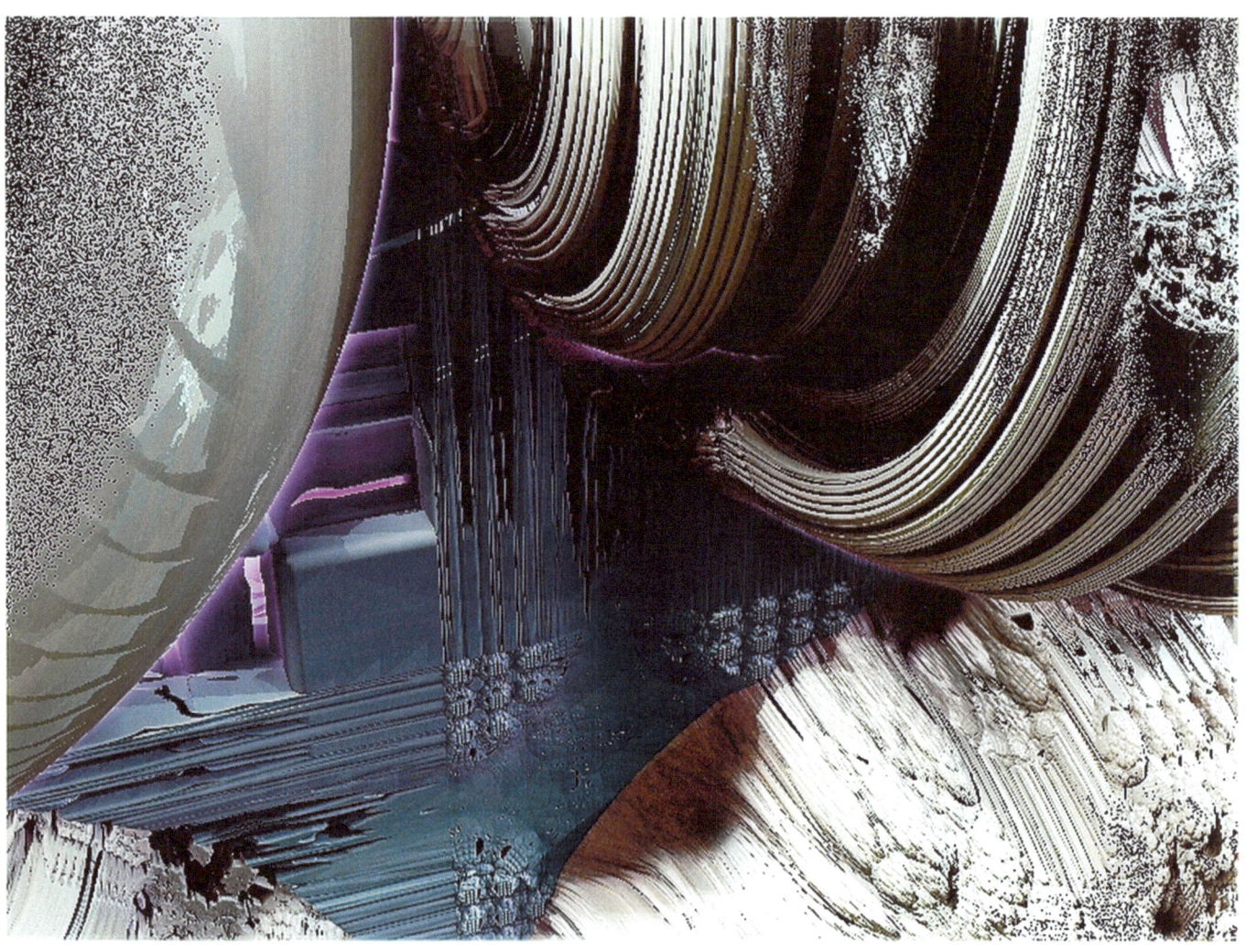

A little more complexity and four interacting equations created this fractal, resembling the inside of a futuristic star ship engine bay.

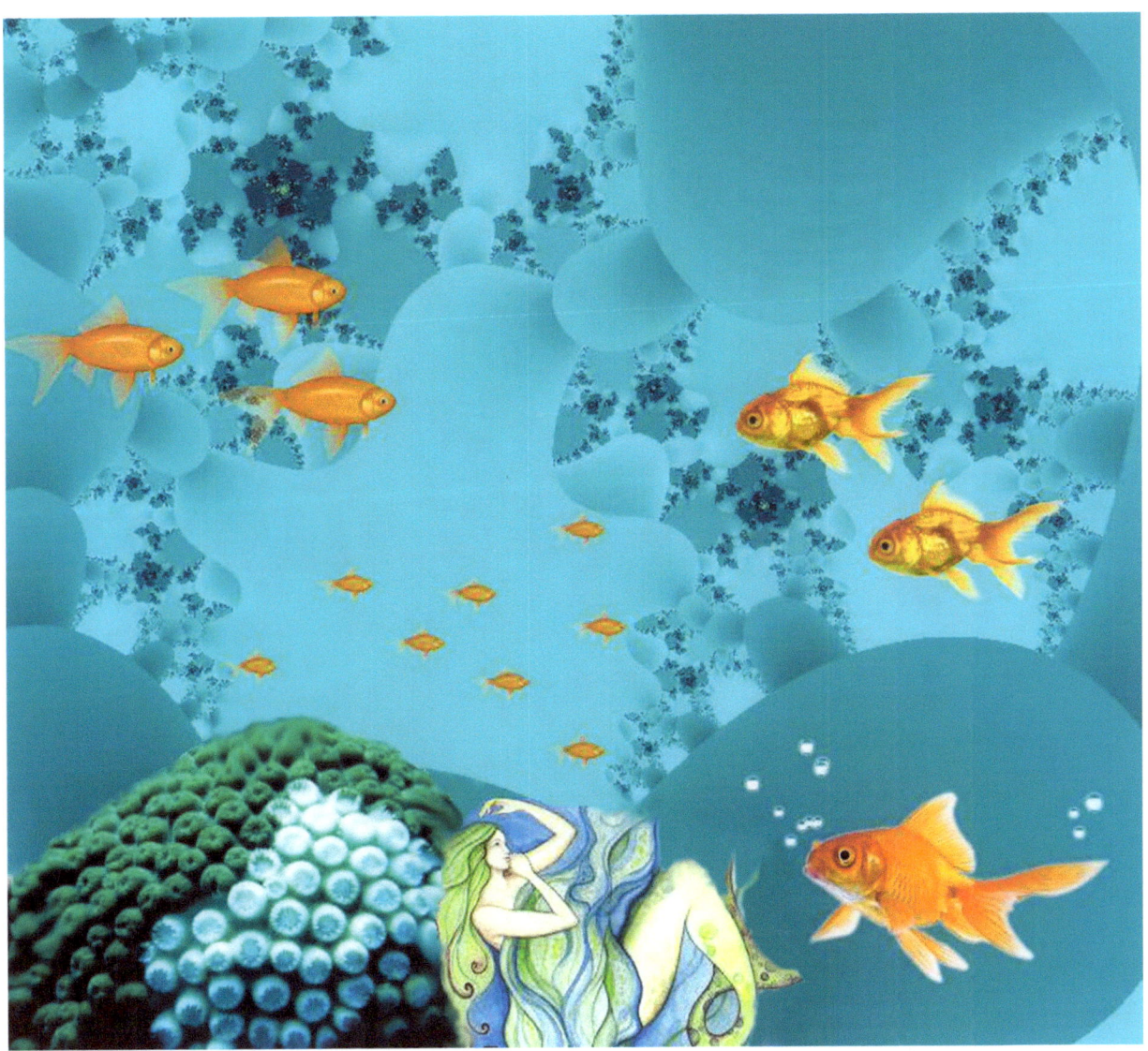

I added a mermaid and some fish to this Mandelbrot to create an undersea image.

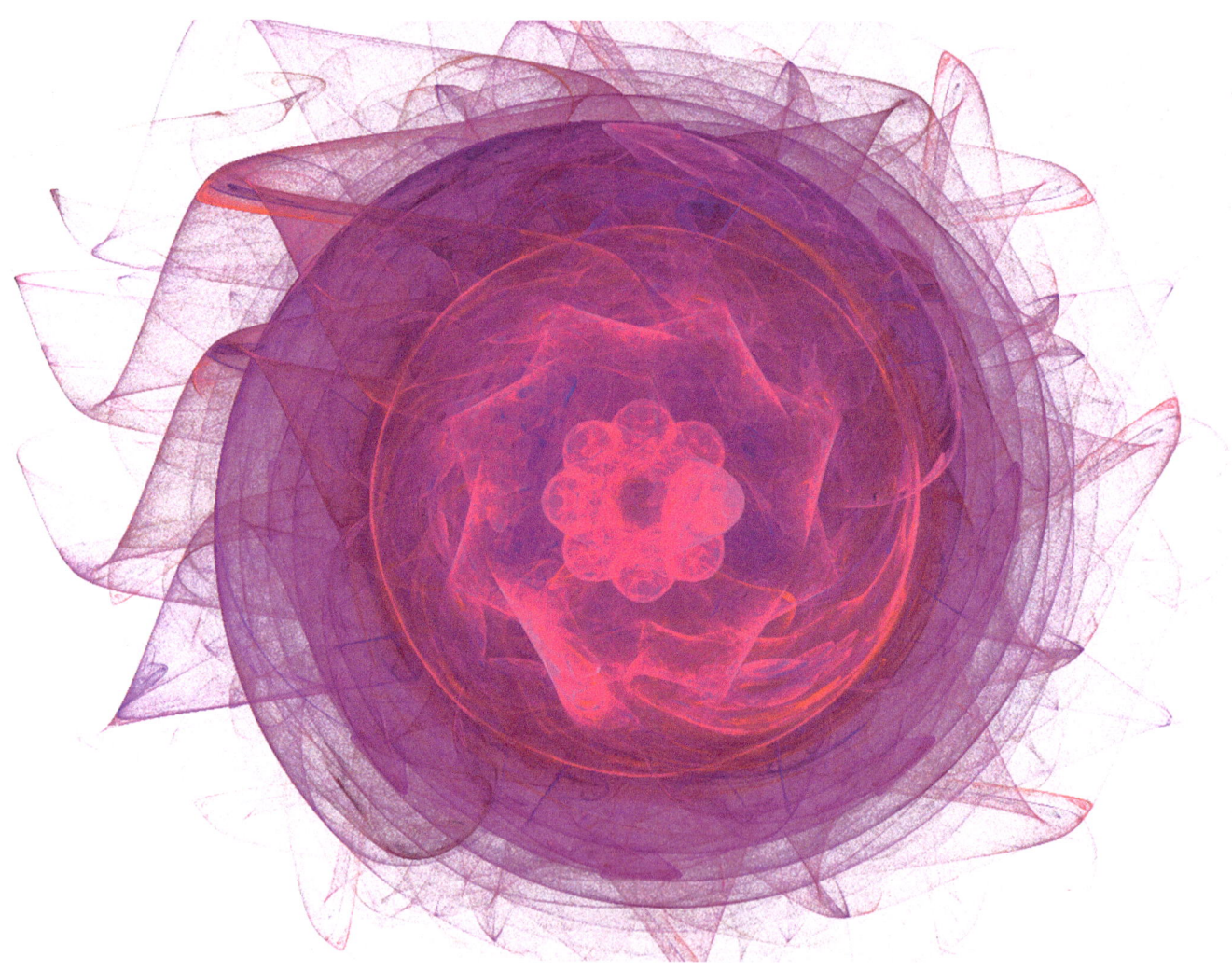

Images can be saved with a background color or as transparent, as this image was made. This image was done with Apophysis software.

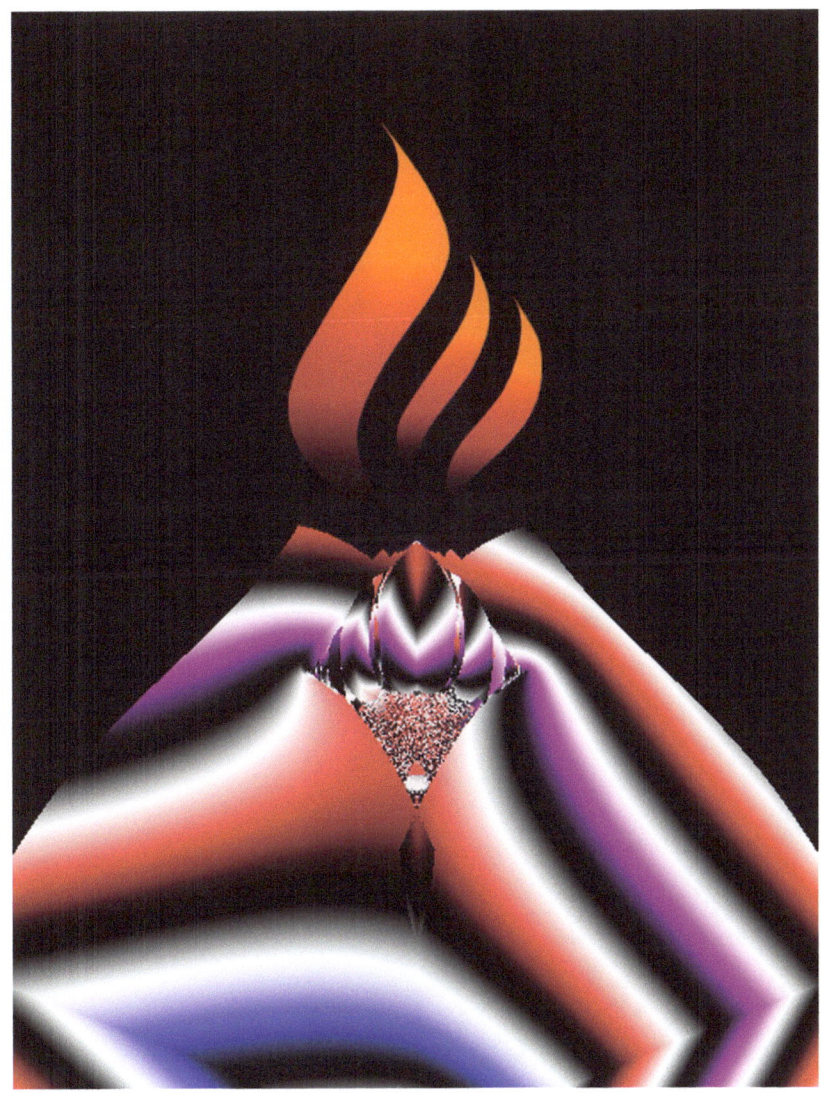

Another example of mixed media. The flame is a vector image created by hand, the burner is a fourth order Mandelbrot fractal.

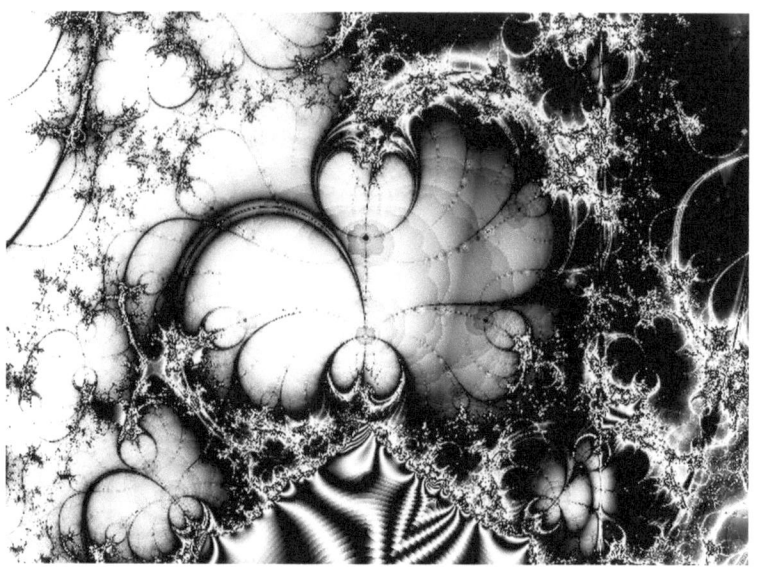

These two black and white images were created with Sterling software

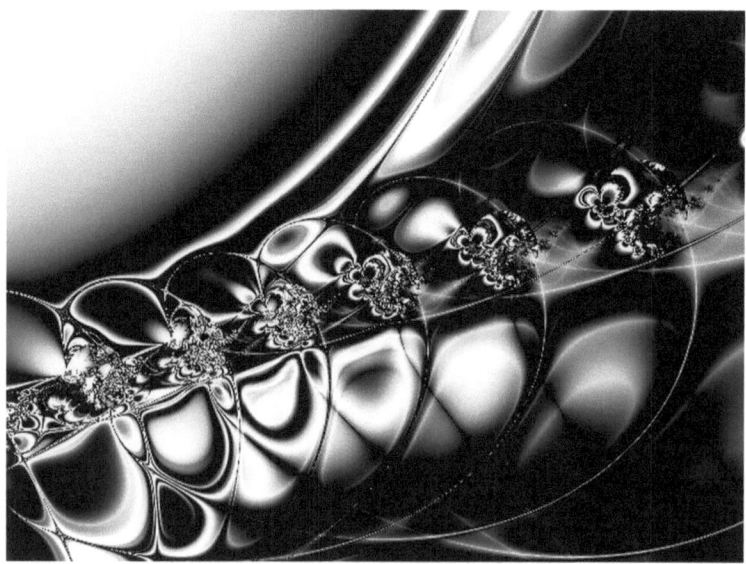

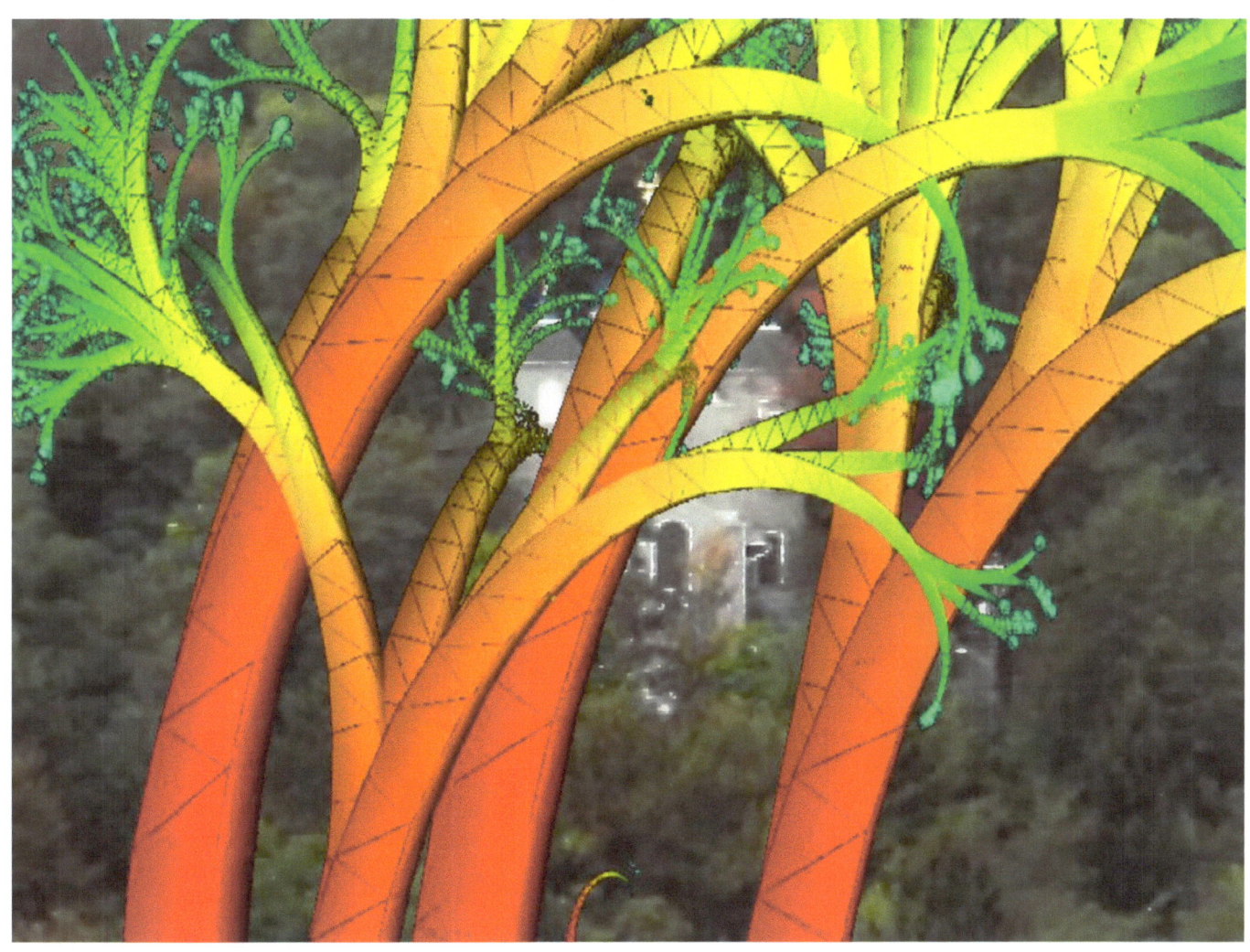

Another fractal overlaid on a photograph of a church in Centralia, PA

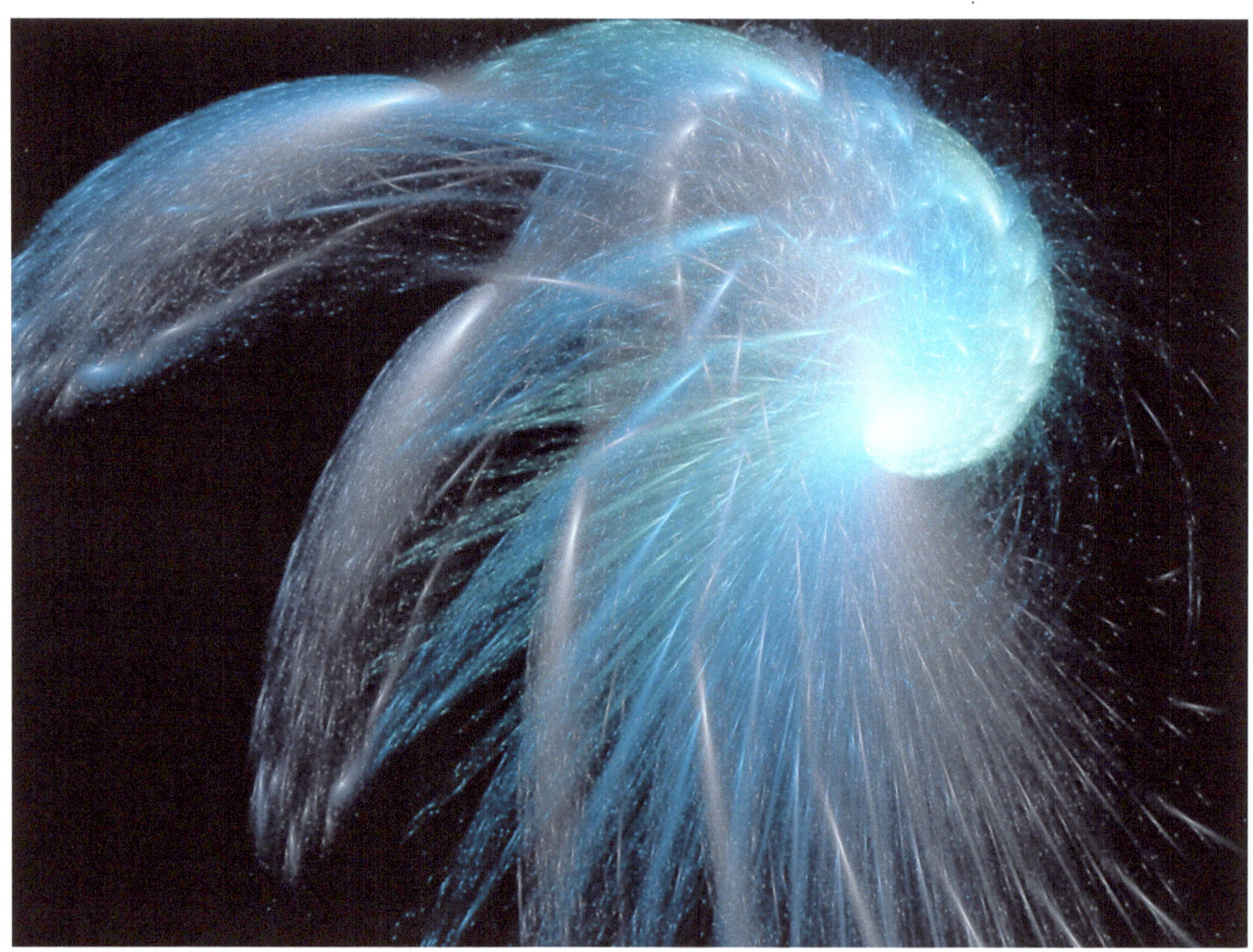

This comet looking image was created with Frost

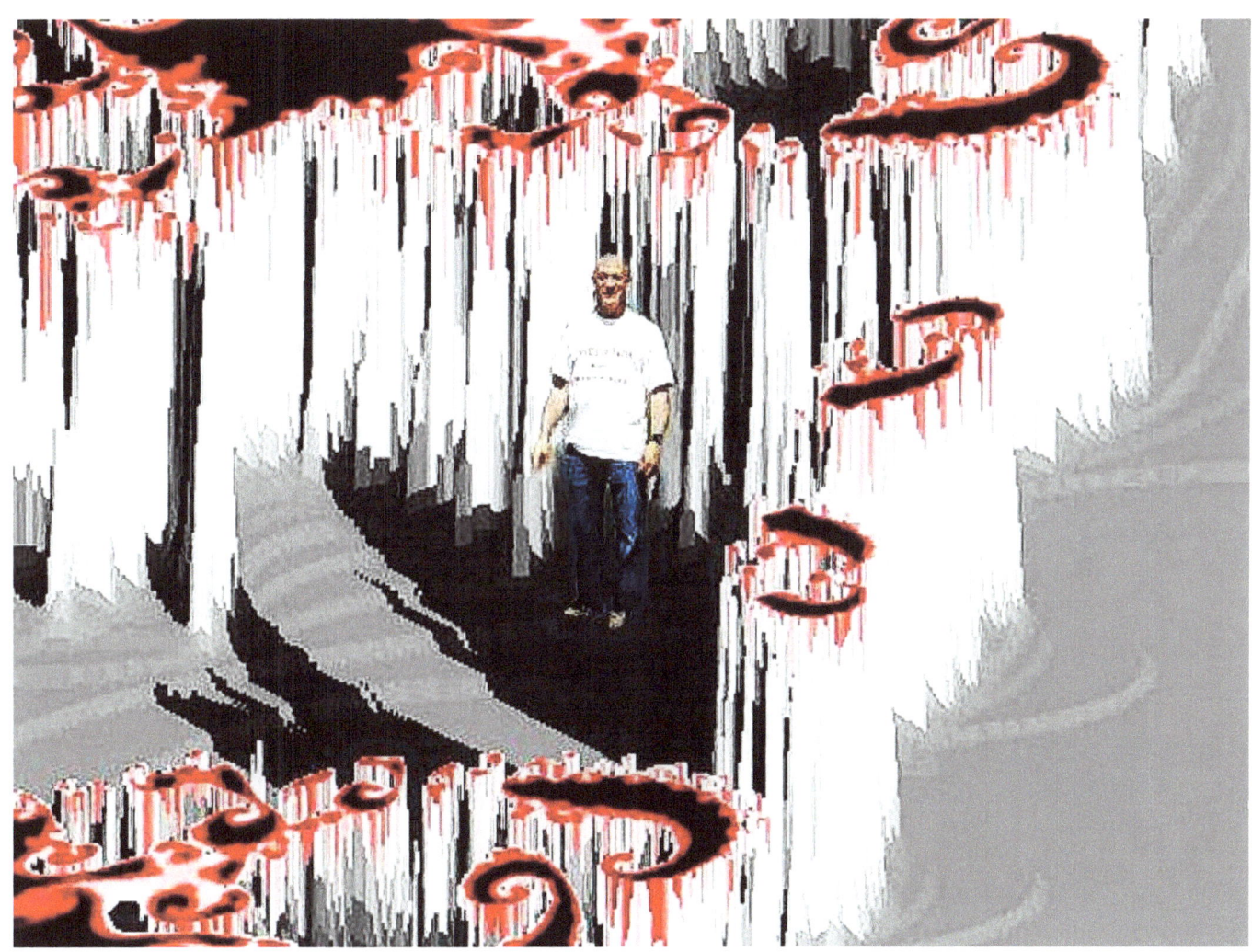

The author in "Fractal Land"

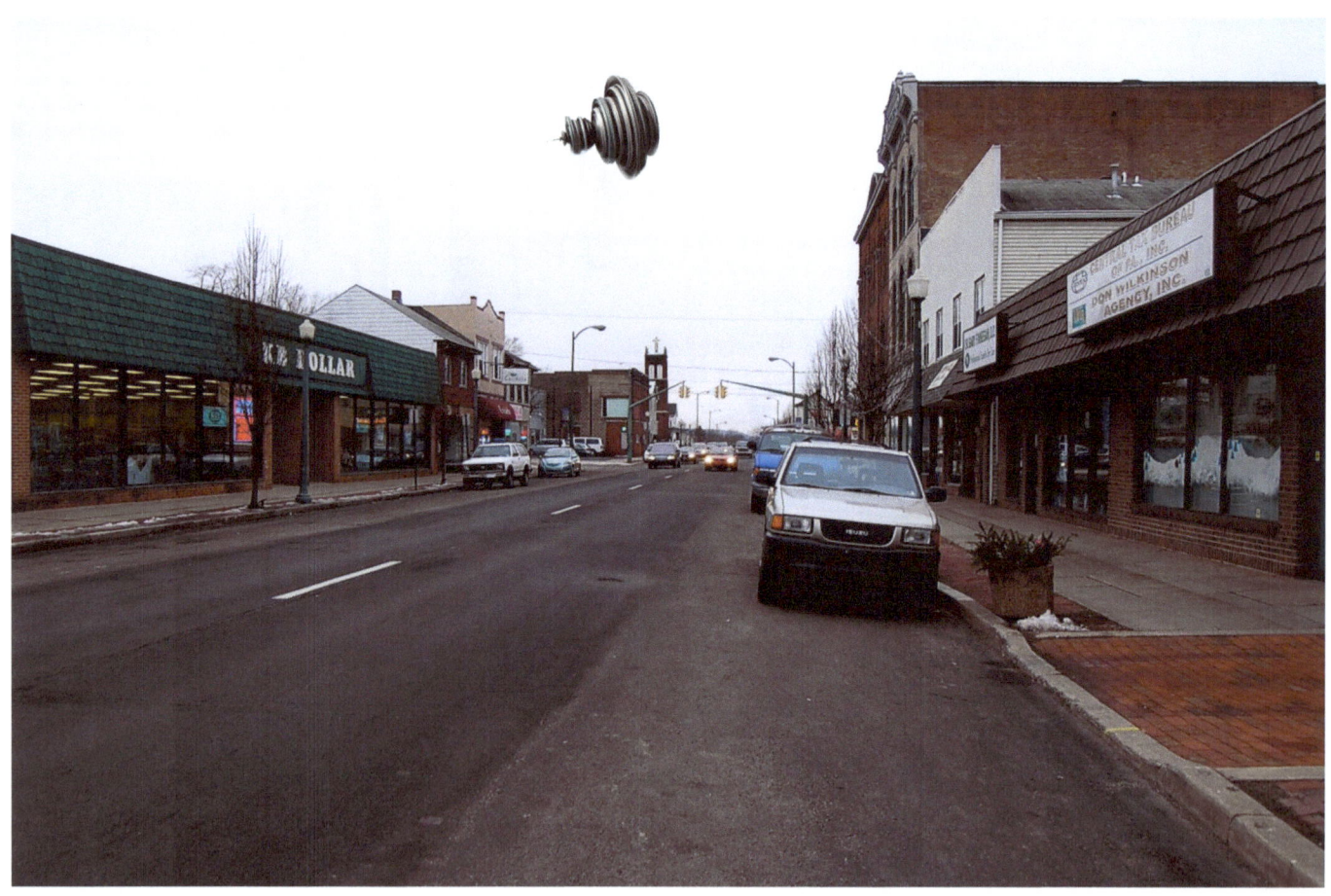

Fractals can be superimposed on photographs or other artwork, in this case a fractal UFO hovering over the author's hometown.

The remaining images were all created using JWildfire, one of my favorite pieces of software. The learning curve is not too bad and there is a lot of support for it. There are also many add-on's for this software.

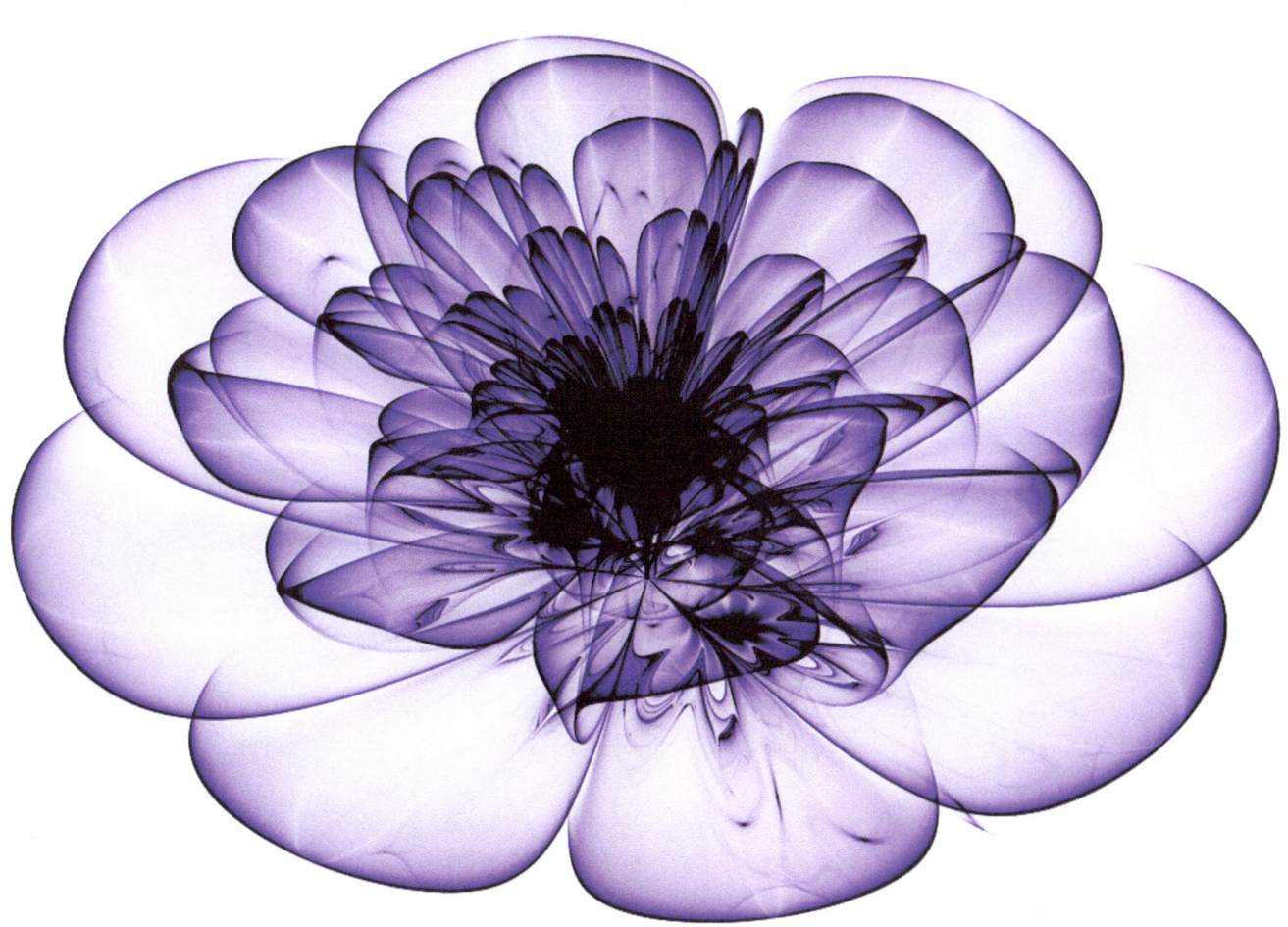

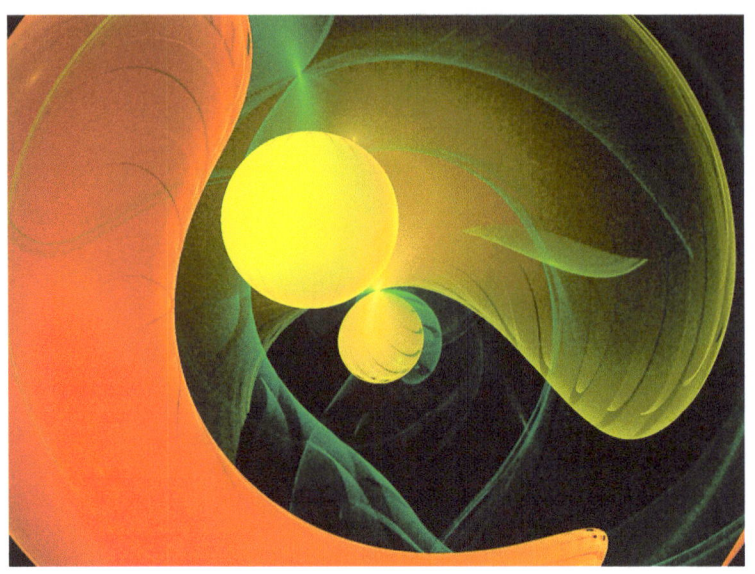

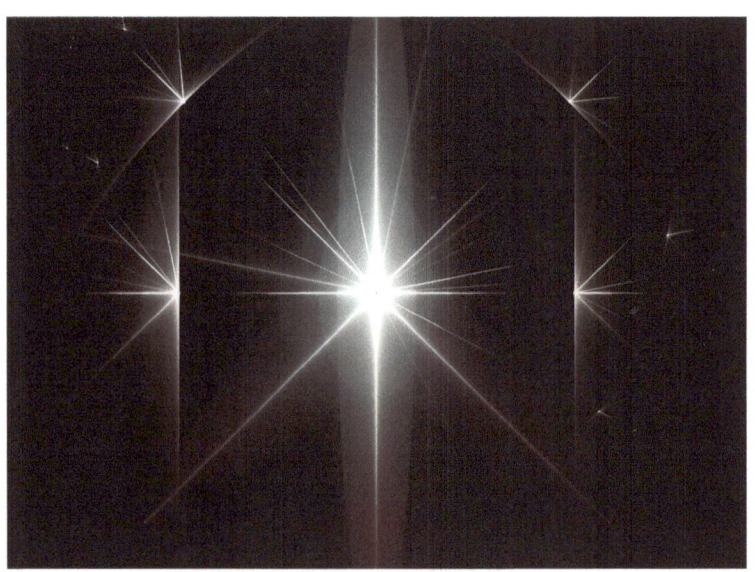

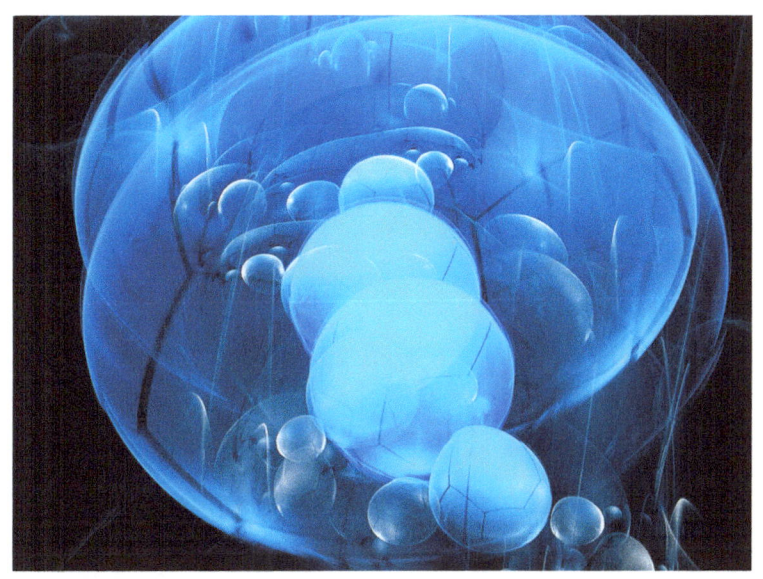

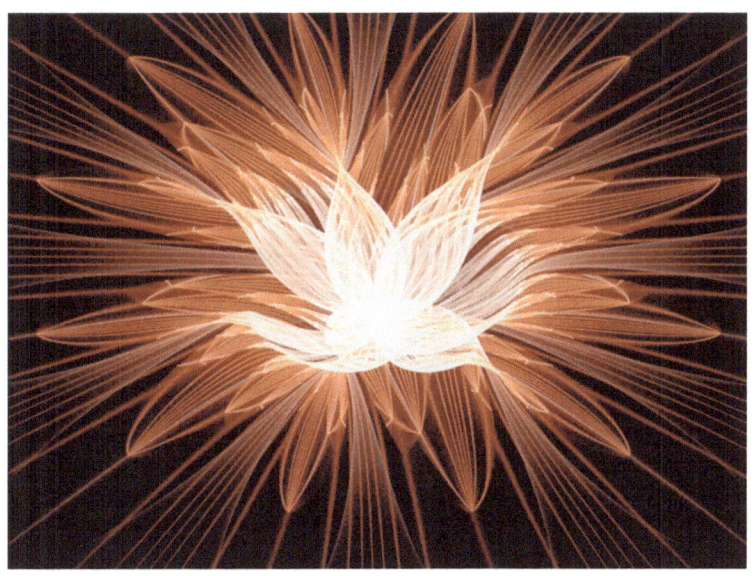

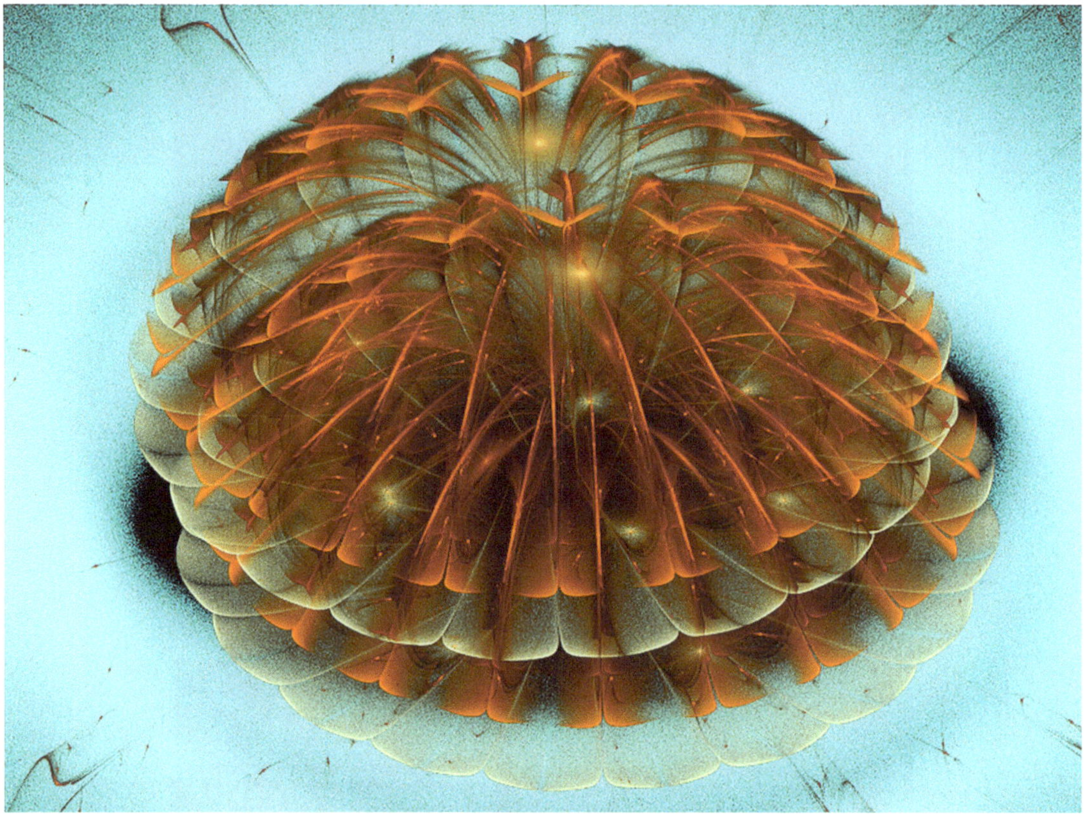

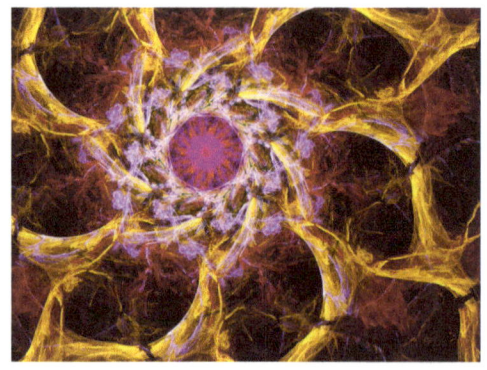

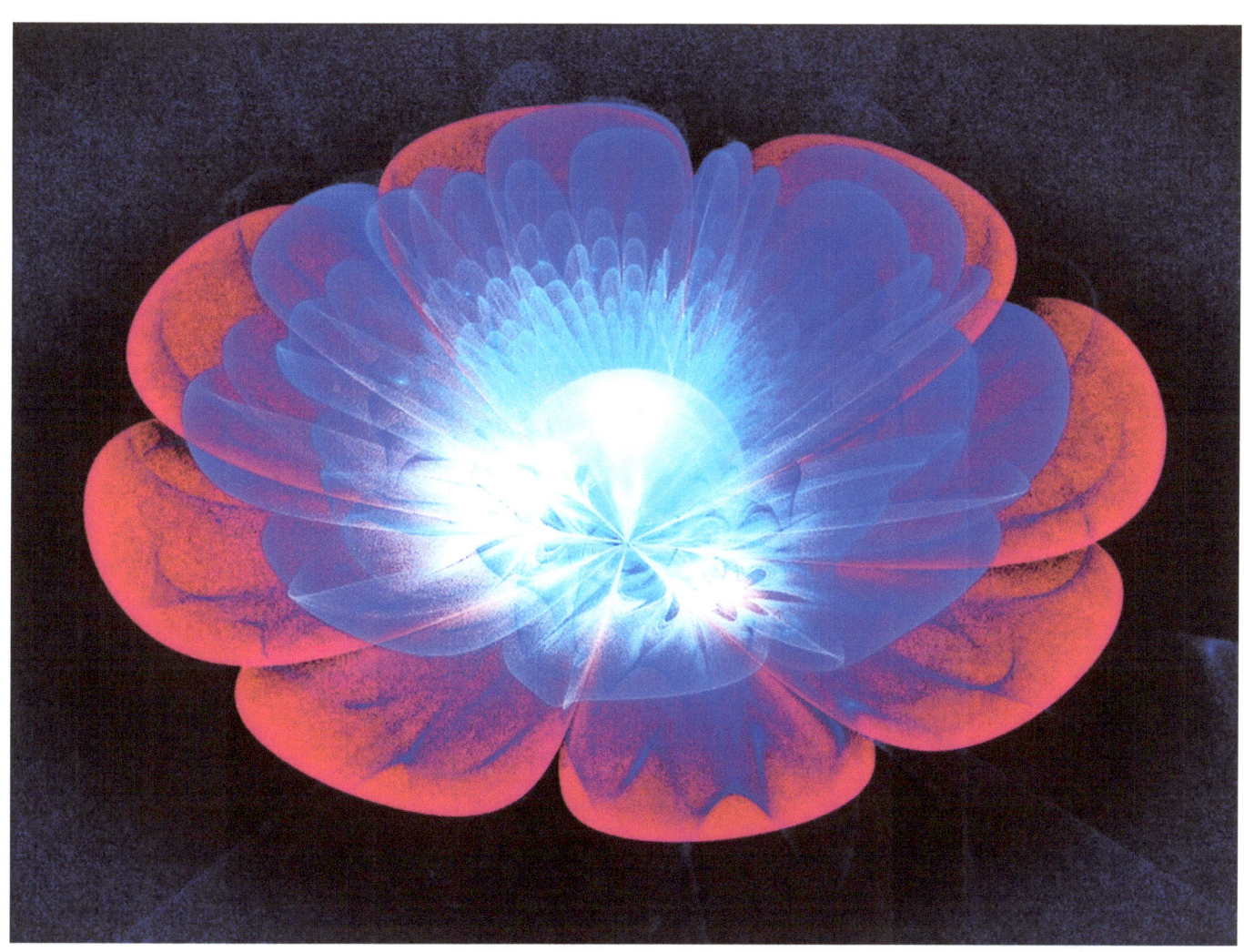

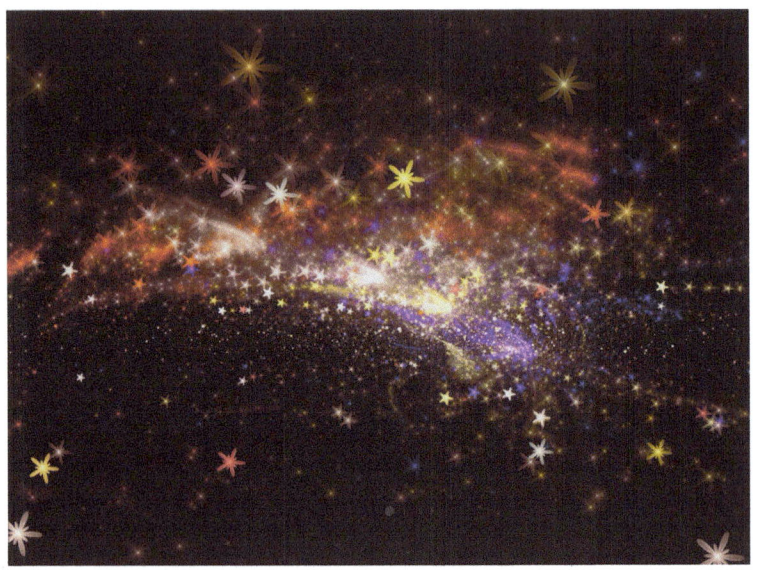

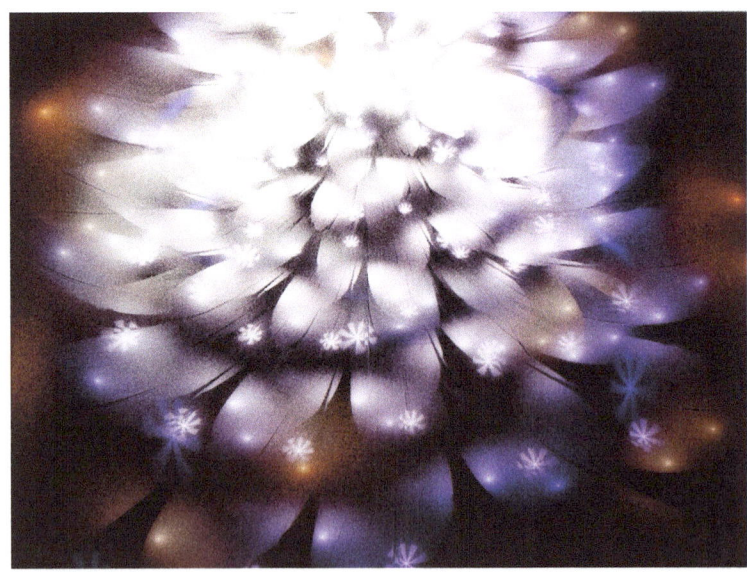

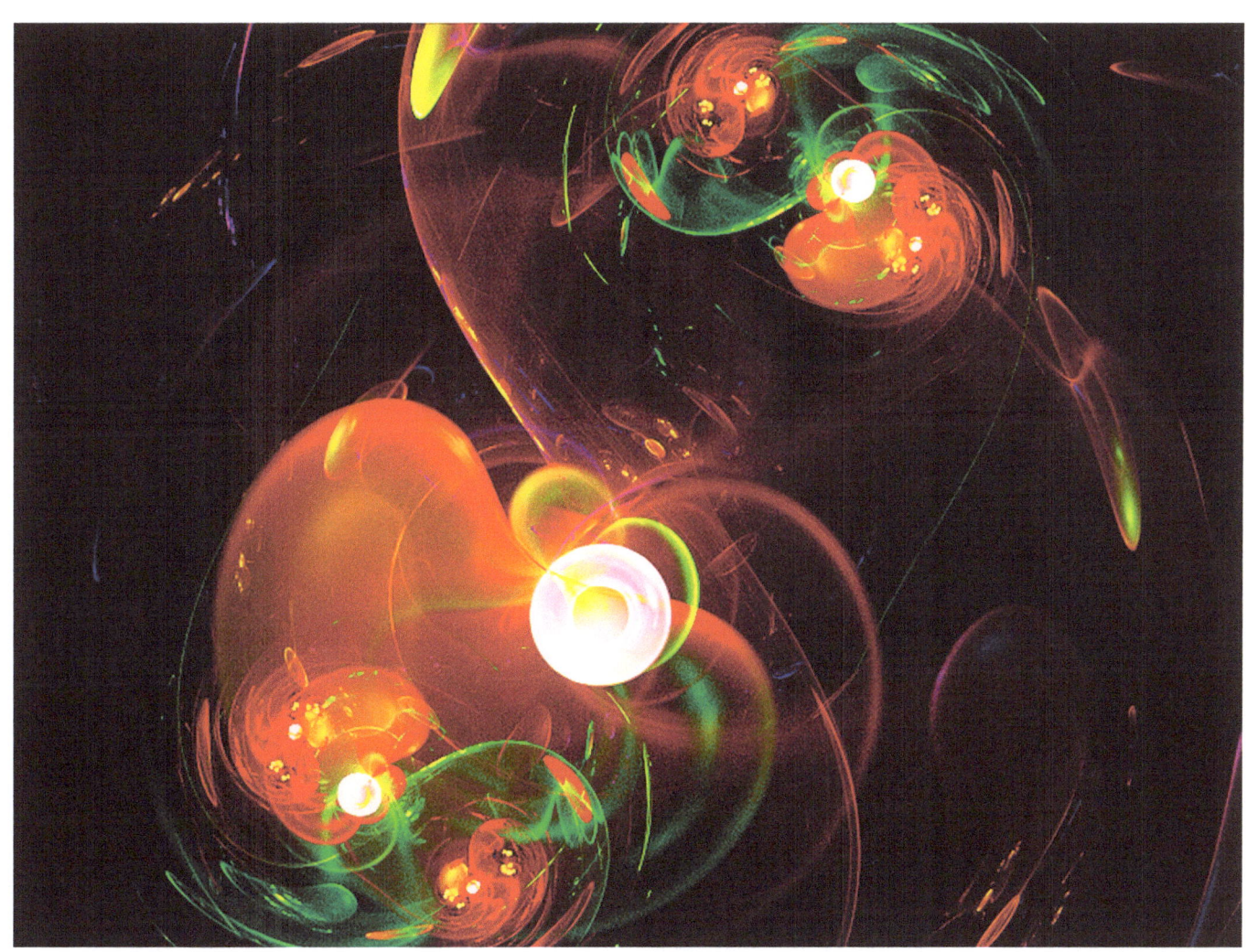

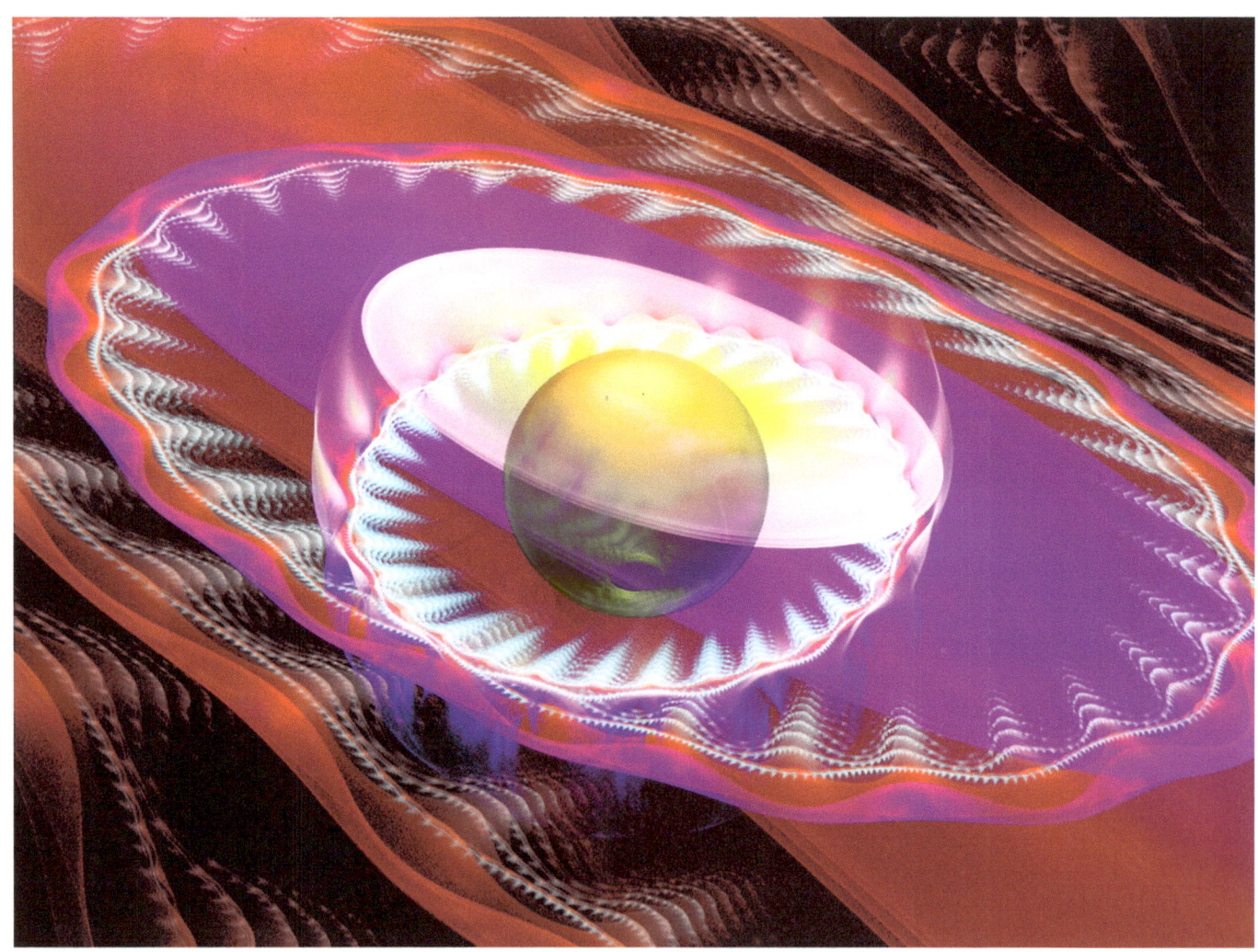

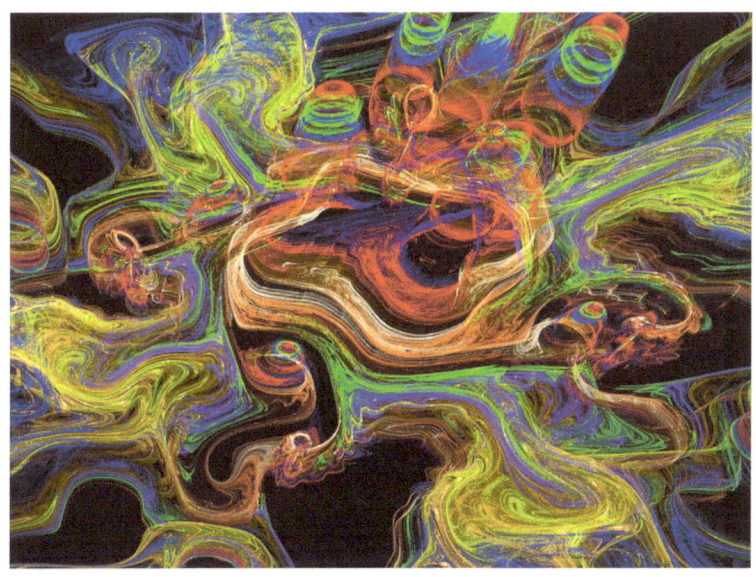

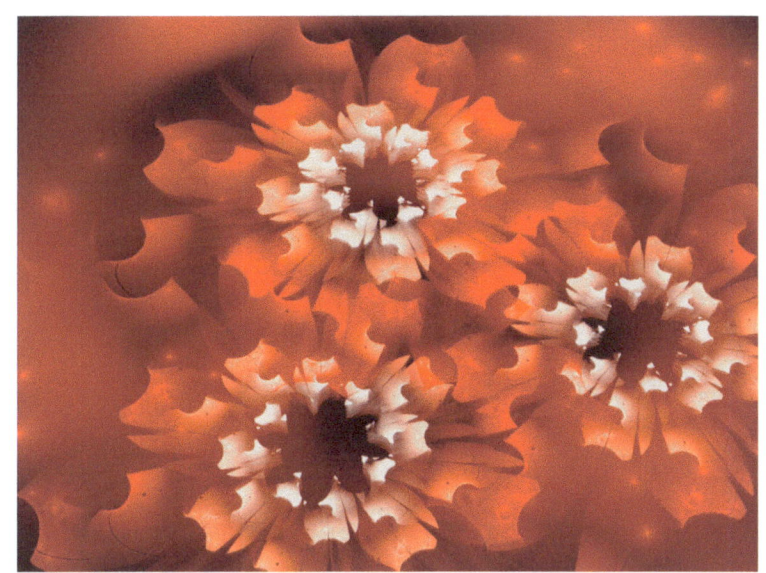

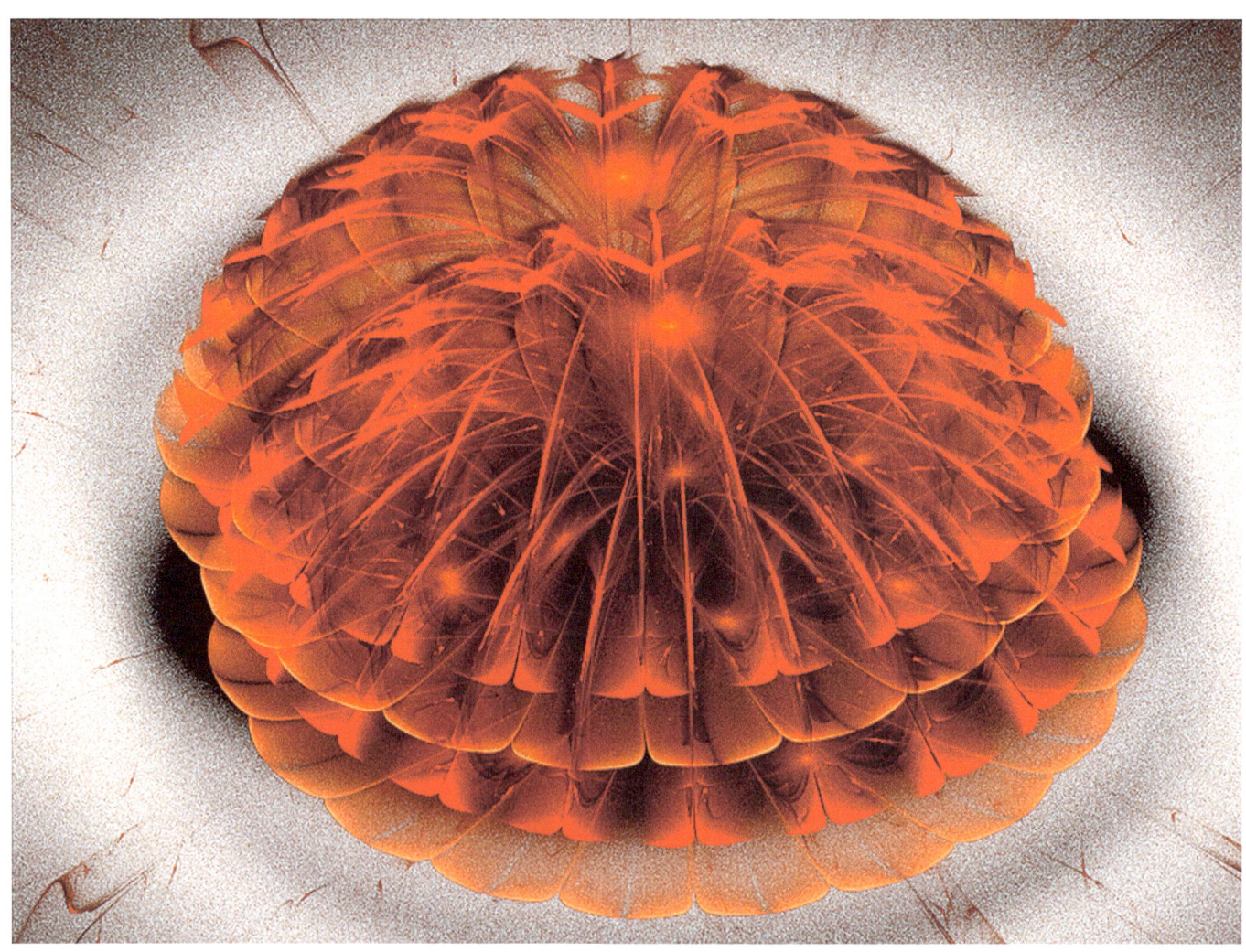

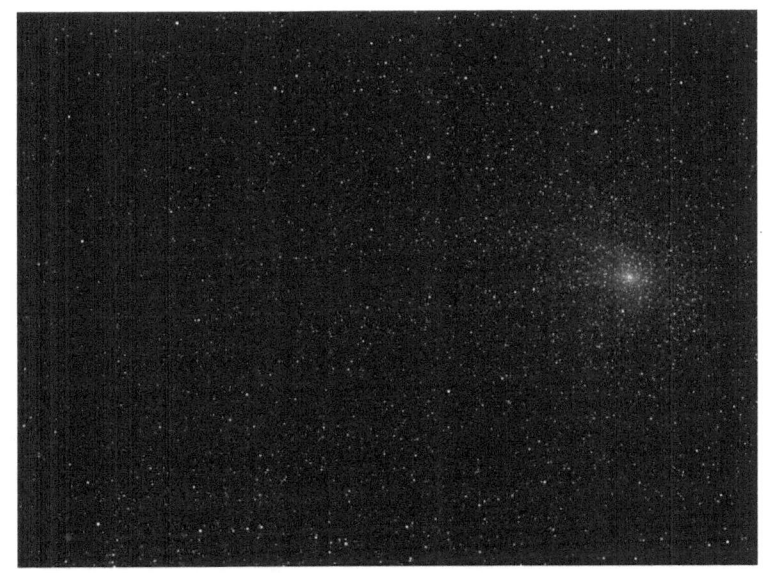

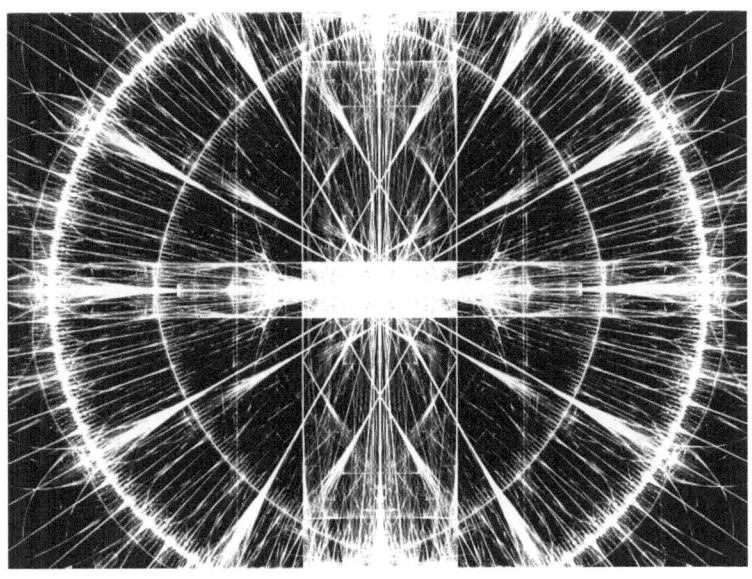

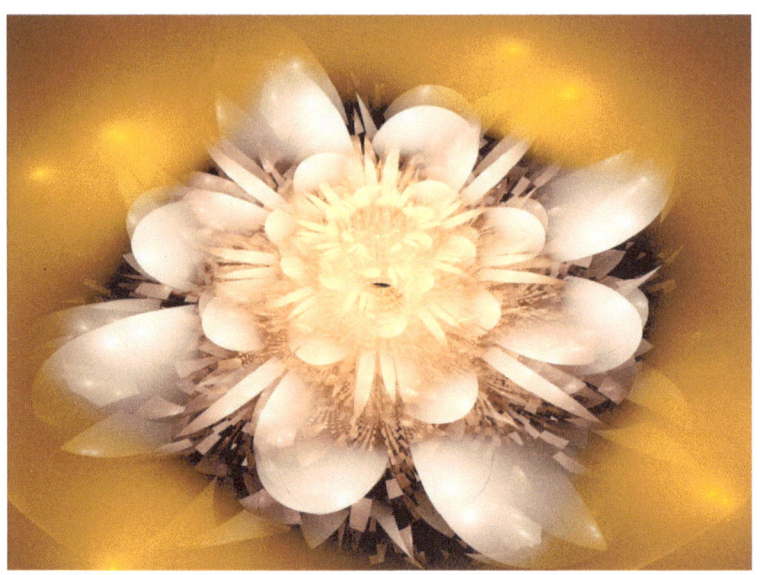

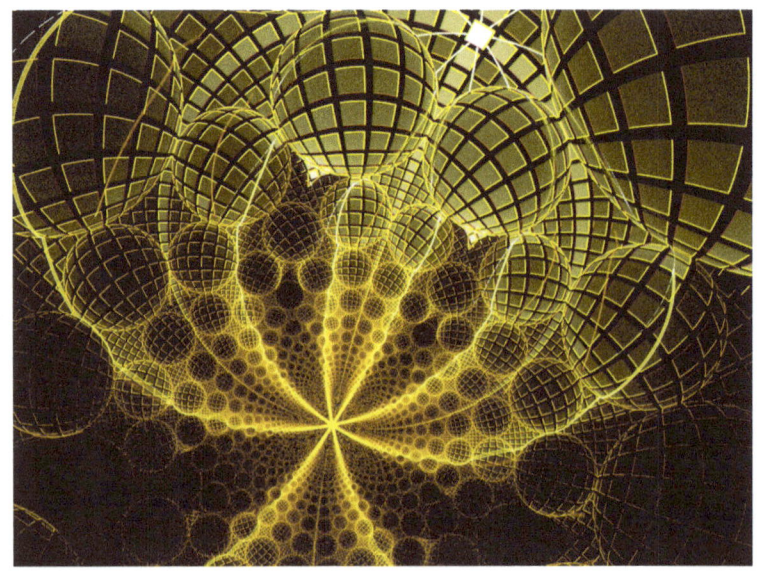

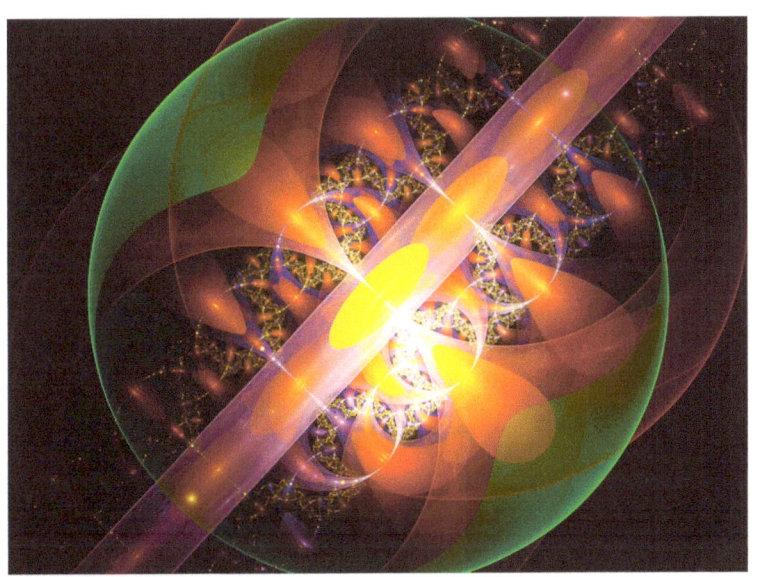

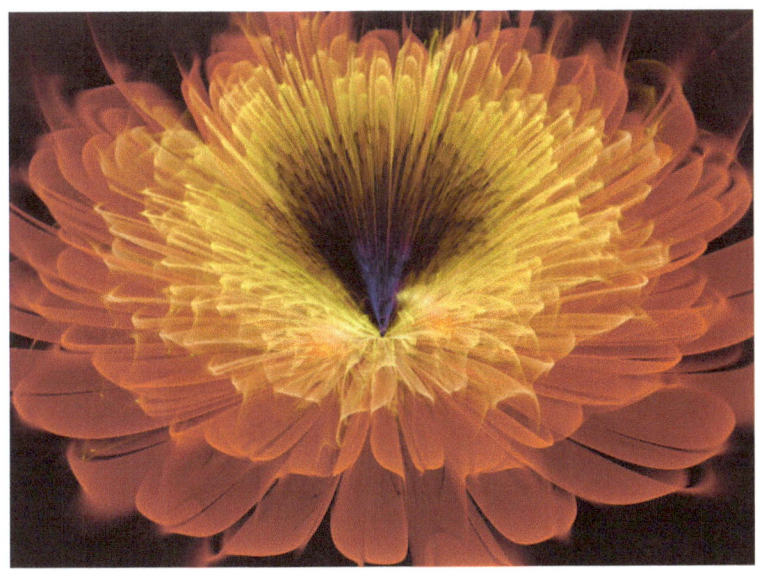

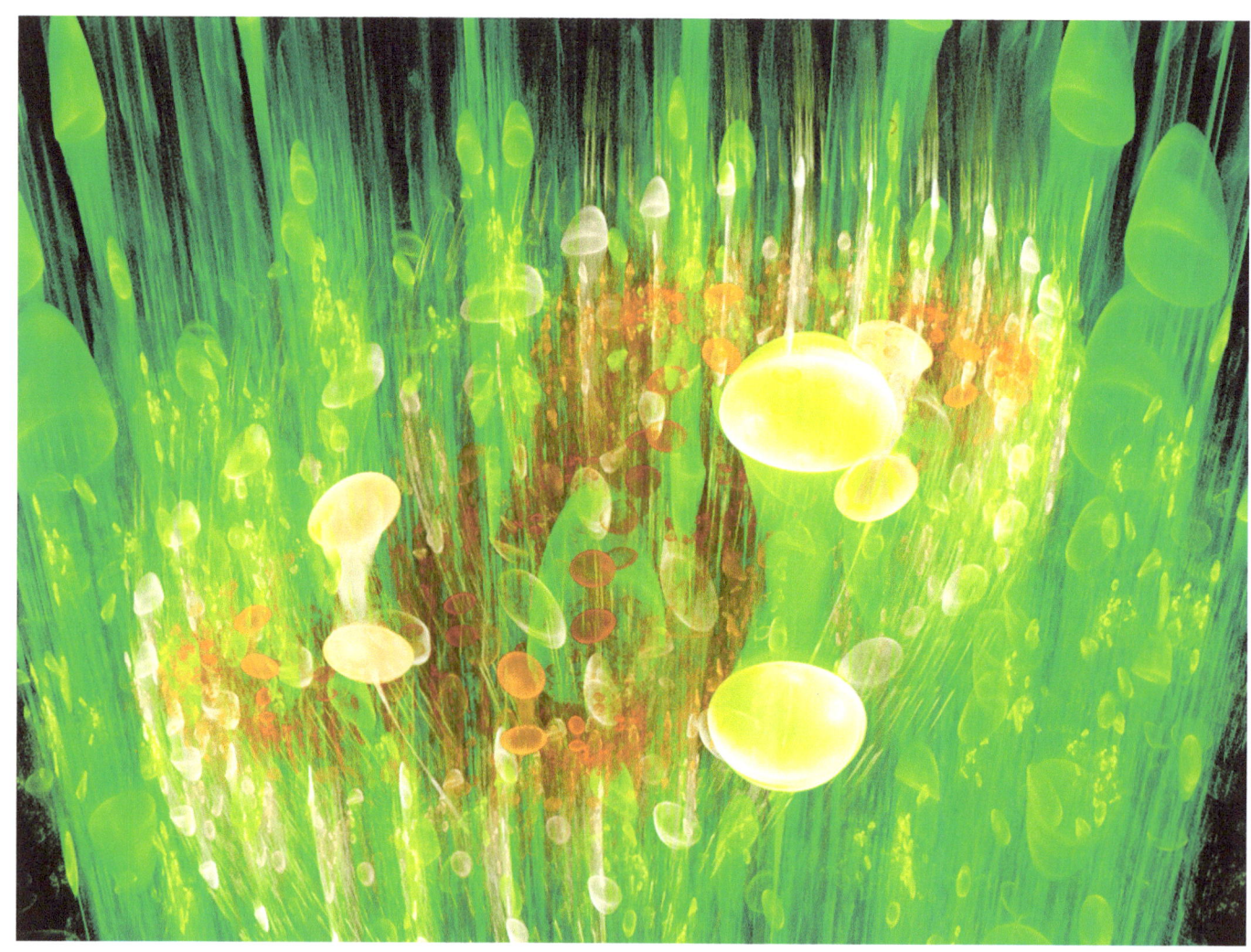

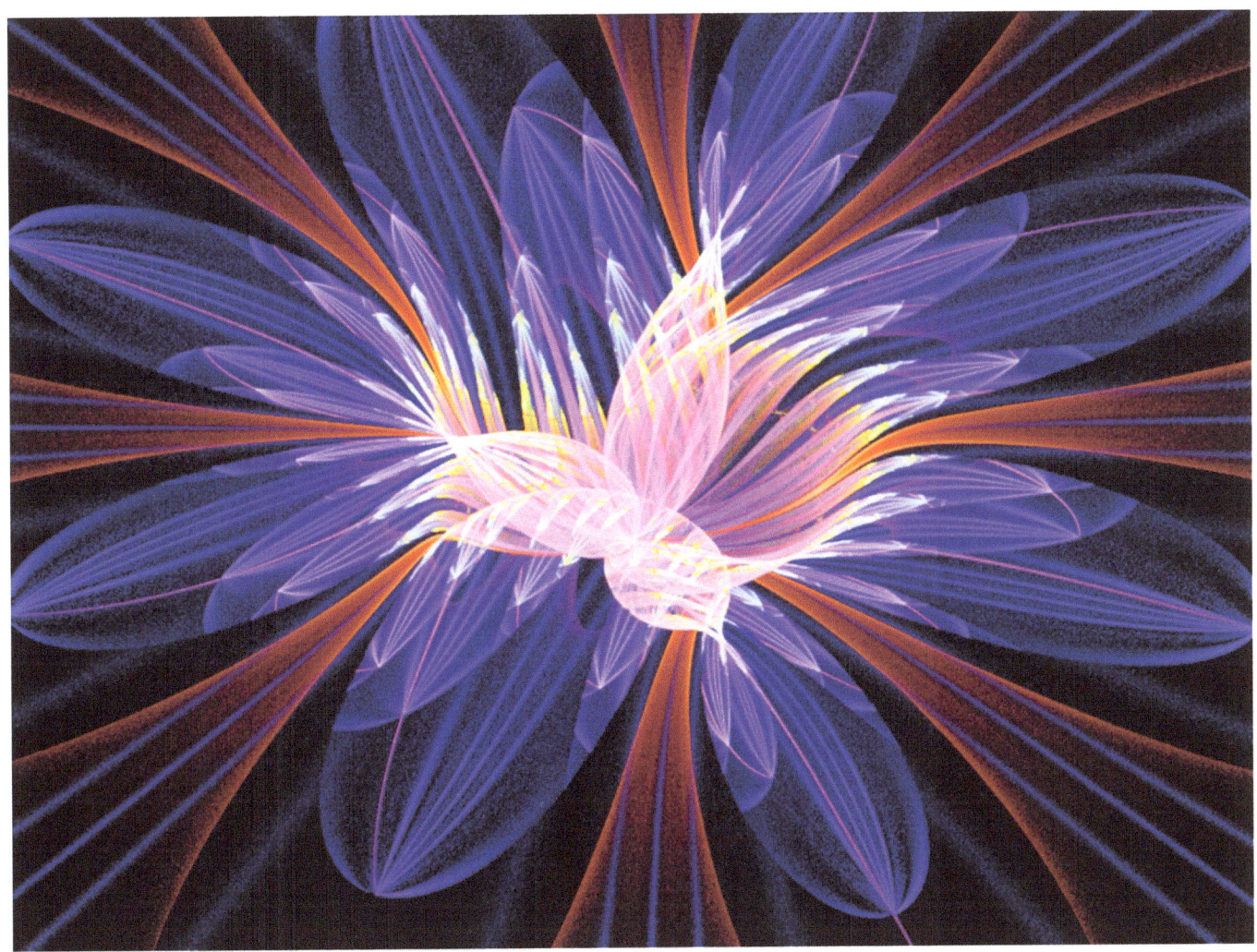

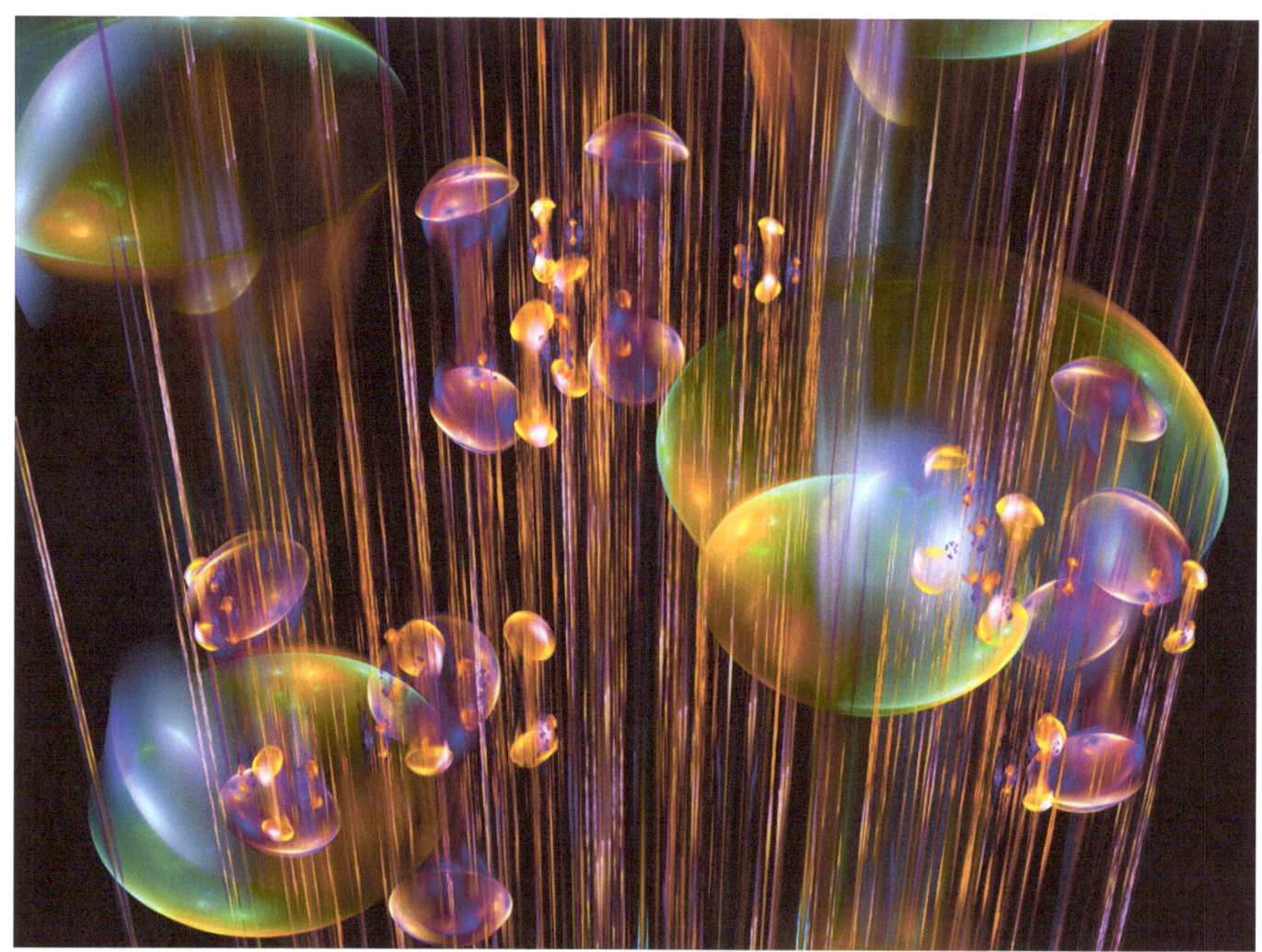

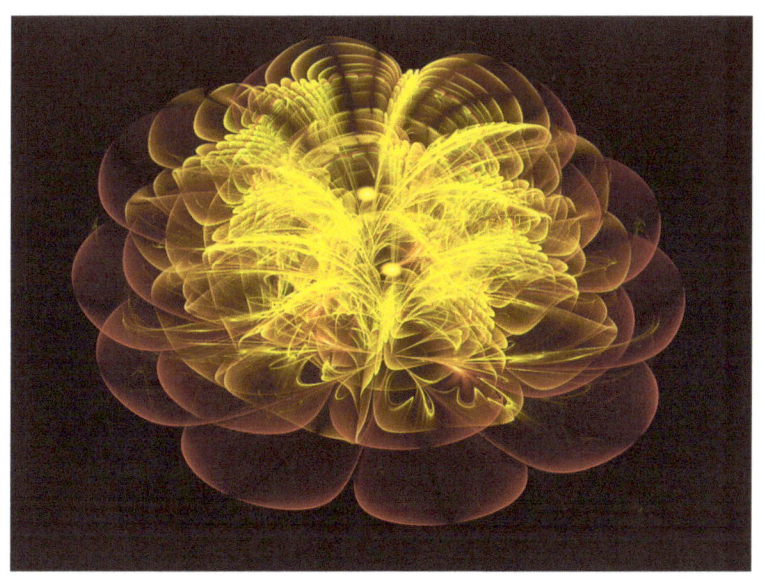

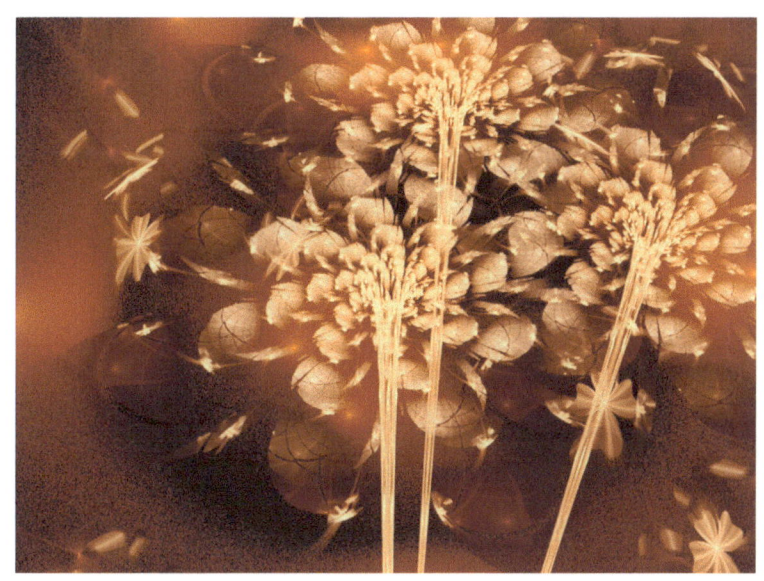

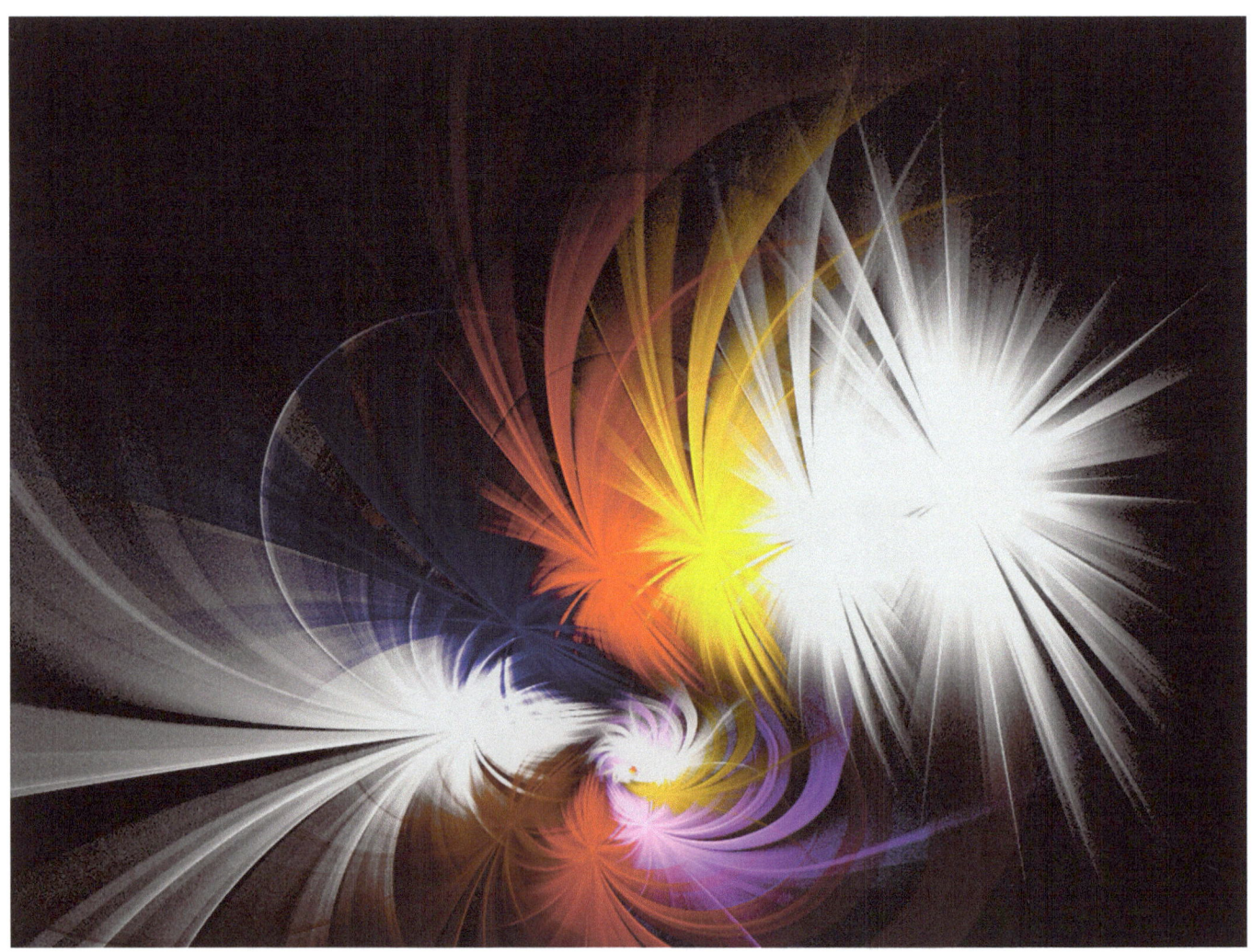

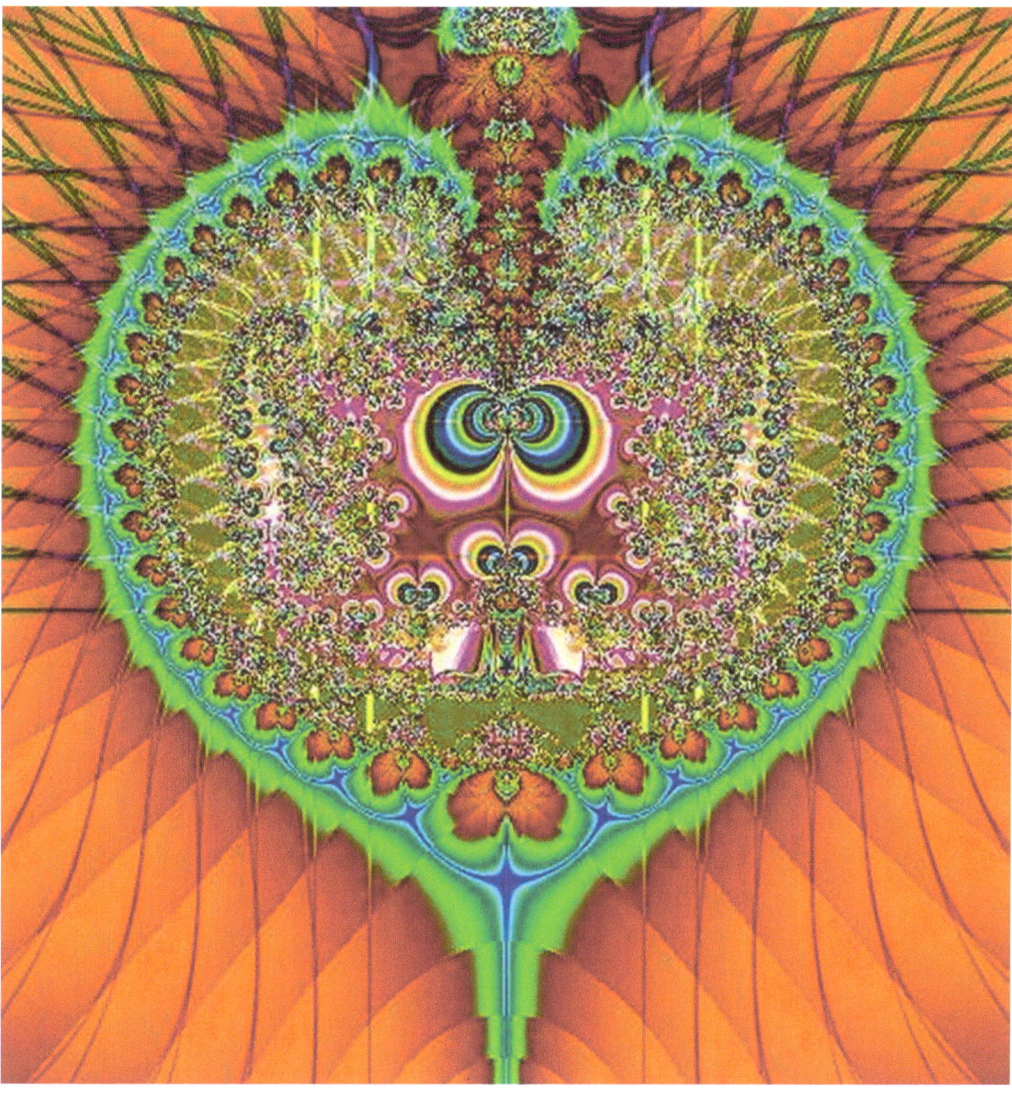

I hope you have enjoyed the images in this book and have been inspired to further research the wonderful field of fractals and fractal art!

Please be sure to stop by Amazon and leave a review of this book!

www.ingramcontent.com/pod-product-compliance
Lightning Source LLC
Chambersburg PA
CBHW050904180526
45159CB00007B/2790